DUMFRIES & GALLOWAY
CURIOSITIES

DUMFRIES & GALLOWAY
CURIOSITIES

DAVID CARROLL

For Toby, Maisie and Amber,
and in memory of Max.

First published 2013

The History Press
The Mill, Brimscombe Port
Stroud, Gloucestershire, GL5 2QG
www.thehistorypress.co.uk

Reprinted 2015

British Library Cataloguing in Publication Data.
A catalogue record for this book is available from the British Library.

ISBN 978 0 7524 6406 0

Typesetting and origination by The History Press
Printed in Great Britain

Contents

ACKNOWLEDGEMENTS

I am grateful to the following people for their help during the preparation of this book: Bernadette Walsh, for technical support above and beyond the call of duty; Bill Lawson, for information regarding Cruck Cottage, Torthorwald; Alverie Weighill, for suggesting several of the subjects included here; the staff of Dumfries Museum; the staff of the Stewartry Museum and the Tolbooth Art Centre, Kirkcudbright; the staff of the 'Devil's Porridge' exhibition, Eastriggs.

I am also grateful to Lorna Adams, Angela Cameron, Evelyn Kelly, Marie McIntosh, Babette Pattinson, Moira Priestley and Pam Purdie for their helpful suggestions. For my understanding and explanation of the charcoal-making process (see 'Carstramon Wood'), I am indebted to Lyn Armstrong's informative book, *Woodcolliers and Charcoal-Burning*. The Belted Galloway Association's website also proved invaluable for background information regarding 'Belties'. For permission to use an extract from *Five Red Herrings* by Dorothy L. Sayers, I am grateful to David Higham Associates.

Every reasonable effort has been made to trace the holders of copyright material. Any omissions are regretted and will be rectified, upon notification, in any future edition of this work. Finally, all the photographs that appear in this book were taken by and are the copyright of the author.

INTRODUCTION

The area covered by Dumfries and Galloway is a large one (in fact, it runs to almost 2,500 square miles). However, it wasn't until I began researching this book, repeatedly driving the length and breadth of the region in search of some of its more unusual aspects, that I realised just how extensive it is.

Dumfries and Galloway comprises the separate counties of Wigtownshire and Kirkcudbrightshire (historically Galloway), together with Dumfriesshire. There are few towns of any great size, the most notable of which is the region's administrative centre, Dumfries. Given the sparsely-inhabited tracts of mountains, moorlands and forests contained within its boundaries, it is not surprising that the population of Dumfries and Galloway is low (the figure is around 150,000, making an average of sixty people per square mile). What is more unexpected, perhaps, is the abundance and variety of 'curiosities' that Dumfries and Galloway can offer. There are unusual landscape features such as the Motte of Urr and the Devil's Beef Tub, together with distinctive buildings including Orchardton Tower and also the Cable House near Portpatrick. A wartime pillbox at Heathhall and a Mulberry Harbour off the coast at Garlieston, not forgetting our distant ancestors' endeavours in creating the Torhouse Stone Circle and the burial chambers at Cairnholy, are among the many interesting discoveries that the reader will make in these pages.

Dumfries and Galloway is also remarkable for its range of truly unique features, including Wanlockhead, which is Scotland's highest village, and the Mull of Galloway, which is Scotland's most southerly point. The town of Dumfries is home to Scotland's oldest working theatre, and Balmaclellan churchyard is the site of the country's first civic war memorial. Furthermore, Sanquhar can boast the world's oldest working post office, and Eskdalemuir has witnessed the development of the Western world's first major Tibetan centre. At Moffat, you can savour the experience of staying in the narrowest hotel in the world.

This book is designed to be 'dipped into' rather than being read as a continuous narrative. However, in order to give it some form, the items in each individual section are arranged – as far as possible – from east to west across the region, although, in a few unavoidable cases there are slight variations to this scheme.

I have made every effort to establish the accuracy of the information contained in this book, and I apologise for any unintentional errors. Where information on a specific topic has varied from one source to another, I have tried to draw upon what I have judged to be the most reliable reference in each case. Finally, wherever 'DGNHAS Transactions' appears in the text, this refers to the Dumfriesshire and Galloway Natural History and Antiquarian Society.

David Carroll, 2013

1

Landscape
Features

THE SCOTS' DIKE

A PART OF THE BORDER BETWEEN ENGLAND AND SCOTLAND

Today, any attempt to walk the three-and-a-half miles of the Scots' Dike (occasionally spelt dyke), is almost certain to end in frustration and failure. This sixteenth-century linear earthwork that forms a part of the border between England and Scotland, stretching east to west from the River Esk to the River Sark, is hidden and obscured by dense coniferous and mixed woodland, which runs along its entire length. However, should anyone persist in traversing this boundary, they may garner some scratches and possibly even a sprained ankle along the journey, as they slowly pick their way through a maze of low branches and the tangled undergrowth.

The Scots' Dike, which was actually built by both the Scots and the English in a joint venture, was constructed in 1552. Its purpose was to resolve the continuing disputes that had erupted between England and Scotland over the so-called 'Debatable Lands'. This was an area running south to north (and almost four miles wide) from the Esk estuary to Tarras Moss, north of Canonbie, and the ownership of which was not clearly established. The Scots' Dike was the means by which this land was carved up between the two separate kingdoms.

A modern boundary stone at the eastern end of the Scots' Dike.

Given its historical significance and national importance, it is unfortunate that so little remains to be clearly seen 'on the ground' of the Scots' Dike. It has been suggested that, originally, there was a stone positioned at each end of the earthwork, one bearing the royal arms of England and the other bearing those of Scotland; if that were the case, these 'terminal stones', as they were described, have long since disappeared. However, an old un-inscribed boundary stone – one of a number that once marked the earthwork's course – can be found at the eastern end of the Scots' Dike, about two miles south of Canonbie.

A modern drainage trench and earthen banks which follow the course of the Scots' Dike.

BURNSWARK HILL

ONCE THE HAUNT OF ROMANS AND MALEVOLENT FAIRIES

The large flat-topped hill called Burnswark, which lies about four miles south-east of Lockerbie, is one of Annandale's most distinctive landscape features and can be seen for miles around. Approximately 940 feet high, it is a familiar landmark for motorists travelling on the M74 and for passengers on the adjacent main west coast railway line. The course of a Roman road skirts the bottom of Burnswark to the south-west, and the hill boasts two Roman camps, together with evidence of earlier occupation dating from the Bronze Age. As a result, it has long been of interest to archaeologists and antiquarians alike.

John Maxwell Wood, in his *Witchcraft and Superstitious Record in the South Western District of Scotland* (1911), observed that:

> In Annandale, the great fairy strength and palace lay in the heart of Burnswark Hill. The reputation of these Annandale fairies seems to have been rather disposed towards evil than good. Young men as well as young women were carried off, the former to act as slaves and beasts of burden.

In his story *Elphin Irving: The Fairies' Cupbearer* (1822), Allan Cunningham mentions how the fairies were eventually expelled from the place by 'Donald

A view of Burnswark from the outskirts of Lockerbie.

Cargil, the Cameronian, [who] conjured them into the Solway for playing on their pipes during one of his nocturnal preachings on the hip of Burnswark Hill.'

Long after the Romans had left these shores, Burnswark may have been the scene of a great battle that took place in 937, known as the Battle of Brunanburh, when the English army, led by Athelstan and Edmund, was pitted against the might of the Kingdoms of Dublin, Alba and Strathclyde. A poem in the *Anglo-Saxon Chronicle* recounts the battle, the actual site of which is still hotly debated by scholars. Many different possible locations have been suggested over the years, but Burnswark certainly remains one of the more persistent candidates.

LOCHMABEN OLD CASTLE
GOLF COURSE'S LINK WITH ANCIENT FORTIFICATION

The remains of a once-impressive castle lie on the wooded banks of Castle Loch at Lochmaben. It was built around 1300 by the English monarch Edward I (sometimes known as the 'Hammer of the Scots') during the Wars of Scottish Independence. As such, it was destined to change hands between the English and the Scots on several occasions over the subsequent turbulent years.

This substantial stone castle replaced an earlier fortification – a motte-and-bailey castle – dating from the mid-twelfth century, a remnant of which can be found nearby on the strip of land that separates Castle Loch and Kirk Loch. (For background information about motte-and-bailey castles see the entry on the Motte of Urr, p. 30). It was built by the Brus family, who were the Lords of Annandale and forebears of Robert the Bruce. Bruce's grandfather is believed to have died here in 1295.

Above: *The mound of Lochmaben's motte-and-bailey castle.* Below: *The summit plateau. Now part of Lochmaben's golf course.*

Although it lies beside a public road, from where it can be easily seen at close quarters, this ancient earthwork is not immediately apparent to the casual eye. With traces of its encircling defensive ditch still in evidence, the mound (or motte), dotted with trees and cloaked in rough grass, is denied the clarity of the classic outline, which can be seen at other motte-and-baileys elsewhere in the region – for example, the Motte of Urr, near Dalbeattie, and Druchtag Motte at Mochrum.

Given its sometimes turbulent history – the fortification was captured by Edward I at the end of the twelfth century – it is refreshing to discover that, in an interesting variation on the biblical theme of 'beating swords into plowshares [*sic*]', the motte now serves a more peaceful purpose. It has been woven into the course at Lochmaben Golf Club, with the summit plateau playing host to the immaculately clipped second green.

BROW WELL

A MINERAL SPRING WITH A SAD LITERARY CONNECTION

The once-popular chalybeate well at Brow lies inconspicuously by the roadside, about a mile south of Clarencefield and on the edge of the Solway Firth. Although dismissed by the Revd John Wilson in his 1882 *Gazetteer of Scotland* as a 'decayed small watering-place', Brow was a busy spot in former times, attracting visitors by the score; most of them seeking restoration of their health from the supposed healing properties of this sequestered mineral spring. In 1796, Robert Burns visited Brow Well during the final weeks of his life, in an attempt to regain some of his strength. He arrived on the 3rd of July and lodged near the well. William McDowall, in his book *The History of Dumfries*, records that 'Brow was then a hamlet numbering about a dozen houses, the chief of which was an inn kept by a Mr Davidson, who willingly allotted the "chaumner en" of his little hostelry to Burns as a lodger' (the inn was demolished in 1863). 'Often, great herds of cattle going south rested for a night in the neighbouring Merse,' McDowall continued, 'while their drovers proved the best customers that the inn possessed.'

However, no amount of the mineral water – which he drank from an iron cup suspended by a chain from the side of the oblong-shaped well – could restore Burns's health. He also tried the effects of bathing in the waters of the adjacent

Brow Well, where Burns tried to regain his health in the summer of 1796.

Solway, but all to no avail. There was an apparent slight improvement in his condition at the beginning of his stay, but it was not sustained. Burns went home to Dumfries on the 18th of July and died three days later. (Hundreds of people attended the ceremony that was held at Brow Well in July 1996 to mark the bicentenary of Burns's death.)

THE GREY MARE'S TAIL

'WHITE AS A SNOWY CHARGER'S TAIL'

There are at least three Grey Mare's Tails to be found in Dumfries & Galloway, but the highest and most famous of can be glimpsed from the A708, a few miles before the Moffat to Selkirk road skirts the shores of St Mary's Loch. This waterfall has the secluded Loch Skeen, in the sometimes bleak Winterhope glen, as its source, and tumbles 300ft before finding its way into Moffat Water. This foaming cataract, which is as 'white as a snowy charger's tail', as Sir Walter Scott memorably described it, can be viewed at close quarters from either of the two well-trodden footpaths that begin near the roadside car park. Despite their benign appearance, however, particularly after dry weather during the summer months, neither route should ever be attempted without stout footwear, nor by anyone who does not possess at least a reasonable head for heights.

The shorter of the two tracks follows an uneven course to the foot of the waterfall, but even this seemingly innocuous path is not without its hazards. Landslips and the occasional maverick boulder are not unknown; the latter dislodged by sheep grazing on the steep hillside. From here, the spectacular sight afforded by millions of gallons of water crashing down from a great height is made still more impressive by the thunderous roar of the cataract's downward progress.

The Grey Mare's Tail from the lower path.

The course of the Grey Mare's Tail.

In contrast to this low level walk, the route on the opposite flank of the waterfall climbs up the eastern shoulder of the Grey Mare's Tail, eventually arriving at Loch Skeen itself. This narrow path, which is extremely steep in places, should only be attempted by more experienced walkers, even in fine weather. There are several precipitous drops en route that have been the cause of more than one fatal accident over the years, but the careful walker who keeps to the recognised path has little to fear when the going is firm and free of snow or ice. However, this taxing walk provides an ideal opportunity to not only savour the waterfall itself, but to catch a glimpse of the two distinct herds of wild goats that roam – but reputedly never mingle – on the adjacent hillsides.

MOFFAT WELL

'NO WATER GOES MORE PLEASANTLY DOWN'

A sulphurous well on the northern outskirts of Moffat was discovered in 1633 by Rachel Whiteford, daughter of the local clergyman at that time. Having previously 'taken the waters' herself in England, she was well-equipped to recognise the nature of the liquid that she found issuing from a spring, which was about a mile from the centre of this small town at the head of Annandale. Her discovery was to prove a turning point – albeit a very gradual one – in the development and character of Moffat, which up until then had been a quiet and unremarkable spot. Slowly it grew into a fashionable and popular spa resort, eventually becoming labelled as the 'Cheltenham of Scotland'.

Thomas M. Fairfoul wrote in his guide to Moffat (*Fairfoul's Guide to Moffat*, first published in 1876) that the water drawn from the well has been likened to that of 'bilge water, of rotten eggs and of a gun newly fired.' These graphic descriptions leave nothing to the imagination, although Fairfoul comments, somewhat charitably, that 'the mildest of these comparisons no doubt exaggerates … in the long run there is no water goes more pleasantly down.' The liquid itself was reputed to help with rheumatic conditions, as well as lung and skin complaints.

The small stone building that houses Moffat Well.

A small pump house was built over the spring in 1738, and at the height of the summer season a procession of visitors could be found early each morning making their way along the narrow lane which led up from the town to the well. Once they arrived at the pump house, the visitors drank their 'statutory quantum' of three large tumblers of water. 'A man of moderate energies,' declared Fairfoul, 'may take his three tumblers without being inconvenienced, but on the contrary braced and appetised, though he should not be in any undue haste to run to his breakfast.' The small stone building which houses the shaft of the well, and which is permeated with the unmistakable smell of sulphur, was restored to its present condition in 1986.

THE DEVIL'S BEEF TUB

'A DEEP, BLACK, BLACKGUARD-LOOKING ABYSS OF A HOLE'

Whether it is the Devil's Punch Bowl at Hindhead in Surrey, or the Hole of Horcum on the Pickering to Whitby road in the North Yorkshire Moors, large depressions in the ground seem to exert an endless fascination wherever they are discovered, and such is the case with the Devil's Beef Tub, four or so miles north of Moffat. Originally called the 'Marquis of Annandale's Beefstand', owing to the fact that it was regularly used by the Border Reivers as a convenient spot in which to hide stolen cattle, the Devil's Beef Tub is a 500ft-deep hollow formed by four substantial hills: Peat Knowe, Ericstane Hill, Annanhead Hill and Great Hill. It also provides one half of the source of

The depths of the Devil's Beef Tub.

the River Annan. Sir Walter Scott, writing in his novel *Redgauntlet* (1824), said of the Beef Tub that 'it looks as if four hills were laying their heads together, to shut out daylight from the dark hollow space between them. A deep, black, blackguard-looking abyss of a hole it is, and goes straight down from the roadside, as perpendicular as it can.' Nothing has altered since Scott wrote those words, and standing on the rim of the Beef Tub today, peering down into the deep depression, can certainly be a vertigo-inducing experience. Scott set his escape of the Laird of Summertrees from Redcoat guards at this spot. 'When we came to the edge of this Beefstand of the Johnsons,' the Laird explained, 'I slipped out my hand from the handcuff, whisked under the belly of the dragoon horse … threw myself on my side, for there was no keeping my feet, and down the brae hurled I, over heather and fern and blackberries, like a barrel down Chamber's Close in Auld Reekie.'

AE

THE SHORTEST PLACE NAME IN BRITAIN

The village of Ae, situated about nine miles north of Dumfries, lays claim to having the shortest place name in Britain, and the pedantic grammarian will be pleased to learn that it is also the only place name in the United Kingdom that does not contain a consonant. In addition to this, Ae also holds the distinction of being the first designated 'forest village' in Scotland. Pronunciation of the name can sometimes pose a problem for those people unfamiliar with the district. Some American friends, for example, referred to it as 'eye' when we passed through one day but, in fact, the correct form rhymes with 'hay'.

The village was founded by the Forestry Commission just after the Second World War, primarily to house the many forestry employees who were needed to work in the surrounding Ae Forest at a time of increasing production, in an era when forestry work was very labour-intensive. The project was officially launched in 1947, but the first houses to be built were not actually completed and occupied until two years later. Even the forest that the village was built

An artistic interpretation of Britain's shortest place name.

to serve is of a relatively recent date, with its 15,000-plus acres of mainly Sitka spruce trees and other fast-growing varieties having first been planted during the 1920s.

Although it has retained much of its original external appearance, a great deal has changed since the village was first created. At the end of the 1940s, and for many years thereafter, all employment – for men and women alike – was in some way related to the forest. This ceased to be the case as increased mechanisation took over and other innovative operating methods were introduced. As the volume of forestry-related work declined, people began to find employment elsewhere, making Ae what it has become today – a village in the forest rather than a 'forest village'.

A wooden carving of Britain's shortest place name.

THE 'TWELVE APOSTLES'

THE LARGEST STONE CIRCLE ON THE SCOTTISH MAINLAND

The Bronze Age 'Twelve Apostles' Stone Circle, dating from around 2,000 bc, lies somewhat unobtrusively in a large field near Holywood, on the north-western outskirts of Dumfries. Its low-key setting tends to disguise the fact that it is the largest stone circle on mainland Scotland (although it is more oval-shaped than circular), with a diameter of approximately 240 feet.

Given its national significance, the 'Twelve Apostles' is not, perhaps, as widely-known as it might be. However, it certainly attracted the notice of the Dumfries historian William McDowall, who wrote in 1867 of the 'tree-covered plains of Cluden, long a favourite haunt of the Druids. There grew the sacred grove in which their district priests held annual synod, and

Above & below: *The 'Twelve Apostles', near Holywood.*

the temple in which they sacrificed. A circle of huge, un-hewn masses of rock still remains, nearly entire.' He went on to explain that there was originally a total of twelve stones, 'all of coarse-grained greywacke [a type of hard and dark sandstone] except one, which is of granite.' It is believed that the weight of the largest stone is in the region of twelve tons. The taller 'Apostles' act as useful scratching posts for the cattle, and provide shelter from the sun and wind for the sheep that populate the field at various times throughout the year.

One of the twelve stones was removed from the site during the first half of the nineteenth century, leaving the eleven remaining stones as we see them today. A local legend suggests somewhat fancifully that the absent 'Apostle' is Judas Iscariot who, according to the New Testament, betrayed Jesus for thirty pieces of silver. Perhaps this particular stone suffered the same fate as nine others, which once formed a smaller stone circle situated close to the 'Twelve Apostles', and which were simply taken away towards the end of the nineteenth century to be used as building material. This was an act of unintended vandalism, reflecting a rather different attitude towards the preservation of ancient monuments than that which we promote today.

CRICHOPE LINN
LITERARY SIGNATURES AND A NATURAL ARCH

This low, natural archway lies on the narrow and often slippery footpath which runs above the gorge of Crichope Linn, near Gatelawbridge. Many people have inscribed their names on the surface of the rock over the past few hundred years, although they must all have possessed a considerable head for heights, as the arch is perched above a deep hollow with churning waters below that could send the senses spinning. Robert Burns is supposed to have carved his name into the soft sandstone here, although I could find no trace of it among the confusion of signatures. (However, that is not to say it doesn't exist.) Curiously, the name of the poet Allan Cunningham, born in the

The natural arch at Crichope Linn.

parish of Dalswinton in 1784, has been inscribed on a nearby outcrop of rock, but whether it is genuine or a hoax is impossible to say.

A slight air of mystery has always attached itself to Crichope Linn; a place which, according to an old Statistical Account of Scotland, is 'inaccessible in great measure to man … [and] deemed the habitation of imaginary beings.' In his novel, *Old Mortality*, Sir Walter Scott chose Crichope Linn as the secluded hideout for his character John Balfour of Burley. In his book, *The Country of Sir Walter Scott* (1913), Charles Sumner Olcott could easily be describing the Crichope Linn of today:

> A narrow stream, flowing through a thick wood, has cut a deep chasm in the solid rock, through which the water has carved many curious channels … I had the pleasure of walking up the stream to the falls through the wet woods, in a rainstorm, without a guide. The loneliness of my situation – for I did not encounter a soul on the journey – added to the mist in the atmosphere, gave an impression, which I might not otherwise have had, of the absolute security of such a hiding-place.

FASCINATING FINDS AT DRUMLANRIG
BRITAIN'S LARGEST SYCAMORE AND SOME ARTISTIC SUMMERHOUSES

The Duke of Buccleuch and Queensberry's estate at Drumlanrig contains a sycamore tree that is over 300 years old and is reputed to be the largest of its species in Britain; it is most certainly one of the most ancient. Although not native to our islands, the sycamore has been a part of the British landscape since at least the Middle Ages, after arriving here from Europe.

Presumably planted around the turn of the eighteenth century, the Drumlanrig Sycamore was probably a mere sapling when the Acts of Union – the joining together of England and Scotland – came into effect in 1707. According to the information board in the parkland setting where it stands, the sycamore's statistics are impressive indeed, as befits its advanced age. Soaring to a height of just over 100 feet, its trunk has a girth of 23 feet, while the labyrinthine root system draws up an astonishing 134,000 gallons of water per year. When in full leaf during the summer months, its canopy covers one-fifth of an acre.

A number of intriguing and artistically designed rustic summerhouses can be found scattered – almost hidden – around the grounds and woodlands at Drumlanrig. Built during the 1840s by workers on the estate, they vary in size and style, with some of them being more decorative than others. Local timber from the estate, such as birch, larch and hazel, was used in their construction, together with heather and moss. Known as the 'Heather Houses', their virtues were thoroughly extolled by Charles McIntosh in his exhaustive *Book of the Garden* (1853). 'Some excellent structures,' he wrote, 'have lately been erected through the very extensive and highly varied grounds at Drumlanrig

The Drumlanrig Sycamore.

One of the 'Heather Houses' at Drumlanrig.

Castle; and so capacious are some of them, that not only the family and their visitors, but their attendants also, can find shelter in them. There is a degree of humanity in having such shelters distributed through an extensive domain, as they afford shelter to the workmen in bad weather.' Four out of the five original 'Heather Houses' still remain, and these have all been restored in recent years. They are always a delight to come upon unexpectedly during woodland walks.

WANLOCKHEAD

SCOTLAND'S HIGHEST VILLAGE

It may surprise some readers to learn that the highest inhabited village in Scotland can be found not among the rugged mountain landscapes of the Cairngorms or West Highlands, but in Dumfries and Galloway. Wanlockhead, a mile south of Leadhills (in South Lanarkshire, and Scotland's second-highest village), stands at 1,531 feet above sea level, among the Lowther Hills at the head of the winding Mennock Pass. James Brown wrote a vivid description of this spectacular route in his book *History of Sanquhar* (1891):

> In truth so high and wild is this Mennock road that in winter it is no uncommon occurrence for vehicular traffic to be entirely suspended, leaving the telegraph as the only mode of communication with the outer world available to the inhabitants of Wanlockhead. In the summer season, however, its alpine scenery makes it one of the finest drives in the district; Wanlockhead comes into sight quite suddenly and unexpectedly. For miles no human dwelling has been visible, nor sound heard save the murmur of the stream, the bleating of the sheep and the whirr of the grouse or blackcock …

Road sign at Wanlockhead.

Dorothy Wordsworth, travelling with her brother William and fellow poet Samuel Taylor Coleridge, recalled their own ascent of Mennock Pass in 1803: 'The road for a little way was very steep, bare hills with sheep ... The simplicity of the prospect impressed us very much; now we felt indeed that we were in Scotland. There was no room in the vale but for the river and the road.' On reaching Wanlockhead, Dorothy described it as a 'wild and singular spot.'

Even measured by present-day standards, Wanlockhead could still be regarded as an isolated community, especially in the depths of winter when the climate can often prove to be harsh and uncompromising in this rugged landscape. Much of the BBC TV comedy-drama series *Hope Springs* was filmed on location in Wanlockhead in 2008.

LEAD-MINING AT WANLOCKHEAD
'GOD'S TREASURE HOUSE IN SCOTLAND'

Lead has been mined intermittently at Wanlockhead possibly since the days of the Roman occupation of Britain. However, it could be said that it was not until the eighteenth century that an efficiently organised and substantial commercial industry fully developed. At the height of their output, the combined mines of Wanlockhead and neighbouring Leadhills (just over the border in South Lanarkshire), were said to account for nearly 80 per cent of all Scottish lead. However, the mineral deposits that were to be found locally were not exclusively confined to lead.

Wanlockhead has attracted many prospectors over the centuries, owing to the fact that gold was discovered in the area during the Middle Ages. This remote

The entrance to Lochnell Mine.

The well-preserved water-powered beam engine.

corner of Dumfries and Galloway could hardly be said to have rivalled the Klondike, but the result of gold-panning over the course of four or five hundred years (alongside the profitable lead-mining industry) have earned the area the title of 'God's Treasure House in Scotland'.

Wanlockhead's industrial 'golden age' spanned the eighteenth and nineteenth centuries, with the lead mines having long since closed for commercial purposes. Operations ceased in 1934, although one mine did reopen during the 1950s, only to swiftly close again. The Lochnell Mine was in service for 150 years before it finally closed in 1860. A section of the mine, known as Williamson's Drift, is open to visitors for part of the year (although it is important to check opening times before arriving, in order to avoid disappointment).

The remains of a nineteenth-century water-powered beam engine stand nearby. It was used to drain water from the mineshafts whenever they flooded (which was not infrequently). It is reputed to be the only device of its kind in the country which is still in place where it was first installed. Declared as an Industrial Monument, the beam engine is in the care of Historic Scotland.

ST QUERAN'S WELL

AN ANCIENT SAINT'S WELL WITH REPUTED HEALING PROPERTIES

Even today, St Queran's Well at Cargen near Islesteps, about two miles south of Dumfries, exudes a slight mystical air; a feeling magnified, perhaps, by its lonely rural situation. Renowned over the centuries for the supposed healing properties of its water, especially where women and children were concerned,

St Queran's Well.

Ribbons and fragments of cloth hanging on trees near St Queran's Well.

the well was named after a ninth-century saint (the many variants of whose name include Querdon, Guerdon and Quergan). Local nineteenth-century worthy, Patrick Dudgeon of Cargen, wrote in 1892 (DGNHAS Transactions) that 'the name of St Jergan, or St Querdon as it is popularly known by in the district, is no doubt a corruption of St Kieran or St Queran, an Irish Saint having many dedications in Scotland.' He added that for 'forty or fifty years since, it was the custom for devotees visiting the well to hang ribbons and pieces of cloth on the adjacent bushes as offerings to the tutelary saint.' Apparently, when the well was cleared out around 1870, offerings in the form of coins dating back to at least the mid-sixteenth century were discovered.

Dudgeon thought that the practice of leaving such offerings at the well had been 'quite discontinued' towards the end of the nineteenth century, but this was not the case. As any recent visitor to St Queran's Well can attest, ribbons and fragments of cloth hang from the boughs of nearby trees to this day. Dudgeon also noted that the Presbytery books of Dumfries from around 1630-40 included several entries 'denouncing persons who resorted to "the idolatrous well at Cairgan [*sic*], called St Jargon's [*sic*] Well".'

One sad and strange incident concerned a lady named Janet Dickson who, in 1650, was tried and convicted as a witch after reputedly taking a sick young child to St Queran's Well, in the hope of saving its life. She washed both the child and its clothes in the water, and then 'ran thrice with skins round thorn tree beside the well.' Later, she used further charms at the child's home but all to no avail.

GLENKILN

SCULPTURES IN A MOORLAND SETTING

The old adage would have us believe that food often tastes better when eaten outside, and I suspect that few people who have enjoyed a picnic on a fine summer's day would disagree. Perhaps visitors to Glenkiln might find that the same principle could be applied to works of sculpture; how much more effectively they can be viewed when sensitively placed in an entirely natural setting, rather than in the sometimes more formal surroundings of an art gallery. Half a dozen strikingly varied pieces of sculpture can be found gracing the moorland acres around Glenkiln Reservoir, executed by three of the world's most eminent artists in that medium: Auguste Rodin (1840-1917), Jacob Epstein (1880-1959) and Henry Moore (1898-1986). The works comprise Rodin's commanding figure of 'John the Baptist', his arm reaching out towards the head of the reservoir; Epstein's 'Visitation', set in a copse of Scots pines; and four pieces by Henry Moore. These are his arresting 'Standing Figure' by Cornlee Bridge; 'King and Queen', perched on a hillside overlooking the reservoir; the somewhat enigmatic 'Two Piece Reclining Figure No. 1', placed beside the lonely Glen Road, and the impressive 'Glenkiln Cross', standing high on a ridge and facing, it is said, towards England.

This pioneering collection of sculptures in a natural setting was assembled at Glenkiln by the estate's then owner,

'John the Baptist' by Auguste Rodin.

'King and Queen' by Henry Moore.

'Two Piece Reclining Figure No. 1' by Henry Moore.

the late Sir William ('Tony') Keswick, between the early 1950s and the mid-1970s. Moore, who was a friend of Keswick's, professed to be delighted by the manner in which his work was enhanced by the rugged Glenkiln landscape, and claimed, towards the end of his life, that he preferred to see his work displayed in this way. Understandably, these figures – which can be viewed in all weathers and seasons – are greatly admired by visitors to Glenkiln and, as Clare Henry remarked in *The Herald* in July 1991, they are also 'much loved by local sheep, who use them as scratching posts.'

THE MOTTE OF URR

A CANDIDATE FOR SCOTLAND'S LARGEST EARTHWORKS

Dating from the mid-twelfth century and built by the local lord, Walter de Berkeley, the Motte of Urr, north-west of Dalbeattie, lays claim to being not only the most extensive, but also one of the best preserved earthworks in Scotland, and is a classic example of a motte-and-bailey castle.

Having already become a feature of the landscape in northern Europe, motte-and-baileys were established in England by the Normans, following the

Part of the protective ditch surrounding the Motte of Urr.

The Motte of Urr.

success of William the Conqueror at the Battle of Hastings in 1066. By the twelfth century, they had made their way north into Scotland.

As a stronghold and defensive structure, the motte-and-bailey castle could hardly be more basic. Typically, it consisted of a flat-topped mound (or motte) which was surmounted by a timber look-out post (or keep). A protective ditch and ramparts surrounded the motte and also the courtyard (or bailey), where the castle's occupants lived in a huddle of thatched wooden buildings. The entire castle was enclosed within a palisade (a wooden fence usually made of stakes). The palisade would include an entrance, together with a wooden bridge – that could be swiftly taken up in an emergency – thrown across the protective ditch, giving access to the castle precincts.

Wherever possible, motte-and-baileys were built on high ground close to a river, and the Motte of Urr, which extends over approximately five acres, lies beside the west bank of Urr Water, with fine views from the top of the sheep-grazed mound over the surrounding countryside. The mound of a motte-and-bailey was often man-made but sometimes, as is thought to be the case with the Motte of Urr, the site of an earlier earthworks was used.

In the great sweep of history, the motte-and-bailey came in and out of fashion fairly quickly, as the popularity of more substantial stone-built fortifications grew. It is possible that the Motte of Urr's defensive role drew to a close around the mid-thirteenth century.

POLMADDY

THE REMAINS OF A TYPICAL GALLOWAY 'FERM TOUN'

The remains of the settlement at Polmaddy are situated within Galloway Forest Park, a short distance from the A713 between Carsphairn and St John's Town of Dalry. A waymarked Forestry Commission footpath crosses the Polmaddy Burn, and winds it way through the scattered remnants of this former traditional Galloway village, or 'ferm toun', as such settlements were known. The path follows a part of the course of the old pack road that once ran between Ayr and Kirkcudbright (until it was superseded by the laying down of the present-day A713 in the mid-nineteenth century). The pack road also formed a section of the old pilgrimage route between Strathclyde and Whithorn.

The buildings at Polmaddy included houses, some of which were so small that the occupants shared a single-partitioned room with their livestock. Other dwellings were more commodious and had byres either attached to them or set apart. There was a mill, which is thought to have been already working in the late sixteenth century (although there may have been one in operation even earlier), and there were corn kilns to dry out the grain. The mill would have been a vital component of the village economy, and no doubt its services would have been additionally employed by the occupants of the scattered crofts in the outlying district. More surprisingly, perhaps, there

Remains of the village inn at Polmaddy.

Remains of a house and byre at Polmaddy.

was also a village inn, which stood close beside the pack road. The inn was reputedly the last building to still be occupied before Polmaddy was vacated and fell silent for ever.

The death knell was sounded for Polmaddy and other 'ferm touns' when, at the beginning of the eighteenth century, the landowners of Galloway enclosed their extensive acres with walls, and turned their attention to sheep farming on a large scale. The landlords decided that there was no longer a place for self-contained subsistence farming communities, such as Polmaddy, and as a result the village and its centuries' old way of life were soon abandoned.

CARSTRAMON WOOD
REMAINS OF AN ANCIENT WOODLAND CRAFT

The old charcoal-burning platforms in Carstramon Wood, a couple of miles north of Gatehouse of Fleet, are simple to find but not always quite so easy to see. Their position is clearly shown on a map at the entrance to the wood (Carstramon is a remaining fragment of a once much larger forest), and confirmed by marker-posts at the pair of charcoal-burning sites, which are next to the footpath below Doon Hill. The platforms can be clearly seen during the winter months, but you must search closely under the encroaching vegetation to find evidence of them during the summer.

A charcoal-burning platform in Carstramon Wood in winter.

The same charcoal-burning platform hidden under vegetation during the summer months.

Charcoal-burning is one of the most ancient of woodland crafts and, although the traditional method has now died out, very little changed in the basic process until as recently as the Second World War, when metal cylinders were introduced to replace the age-old kilns. These consisted of a chimney or central flue made by piling up logs – known as 'cords' – in the shape of a triangle. This was the material to be converted into charcoal. When the flue was roughly 6 feet high, pieces of timber were laid around it vertically so that the kiln grew gradually outwards, forming an ever-widening diameter until it reached the ground. Leaving the flue free, roof-pieces were added, before a thatch of twigs, bracken and earth was laid on the outside of the kiln for maximum insulation. Traditionally, a 'burn' would take around three to five days and nights, during which the charcoal-burner (usually working with a mate) would keep constant vigil, patching the outer walls of the kiln and regulating the air-flow as required. To save time, as one kiln was burning the next would be constructed nearby, in what was, in effect, a continual process; hence the pair of charcoal-burning platforms in Carstramon Wood. The charcoal that was produced here in the nineteenth century was used to supply the iron, brass and copper-smelting industries.

CAIRNHOLY I AND II

CHAMBERED TOMBS WITH A POSSIBLE ROYAL CONNECTION

The landscape of Dumfries and Galloway is generously peppered with prehistoric remains of all shapes and sizes, but the chambered tombs of Cairnholy I and II, situated on rising ground above Kirkdale Glen and overlooking Wigtown Bay, are certainly among the region's most interesting examples of this kind. Cairnholy II lies further along the farm track that winds up from Cairnholy I. Each of the cairns would have been established and used principally as a burial place for members of the Neolithic farming community, who would have populated this coastal part of the region between four and six thousand years ago. Both of these cairns may also have served as a place of ceremony and worship.

As is so often the case with antiquities of this kind, fact and legend become intertwined to such a degree that it can become difficult to separate the two. For example, it has been claimed by some

Cairnholy I.

Cairnholy II.

antiquarians that Cairnholy II is also one of the supposed burial sites of the ancient, possibly mythical, Scottish king Galdus, who, according to James Denniston in *Legends of Galloway* (1825), was 'a sovereign who made some noise in the fabulous era of our history … who fell in a bloody battle fought against the Picts. But against this we would object the posthumous ubiquity of "King Galdus", whose place of sepulture [*sic*] has been, with equal show of probability, claimed by the antiquarians of the county of Wigtown, who assert that he was buried at the Standing Stones of Torhouse in the parish of Wigtown.'

Excavation work carried out at both Cairnholy I and II just after the Second World War yielded some interesting finds, including an arrowhead and part of an axe, among other objects. Of human remains, however, there was apparently little or no trace, thus making it difficult to explain in what manner the burials at these sites were conducted.

TORHOUSE STONE CIRCLE
ONE OF BRITAIN'S BEST-PRESERVED STONE CIRCLES

The Torhouse, or Torhousekie, Stone Circle lies in the remote and peaceful Bladnoch valley, a few miles west of Wigtown. Dating from around 2,000 BC, this Bronze Age monument, set in a slightly elevated position, is an example of an archetypal stone circle, although, upon closer inspection, it is clear that the

Torhouse Stone Circle.

King Galdus's Tomb.

circle is in fact irregular in shape. Not surprisingly, after the passage of 4,000 years, the original purpose of the circle is unclear, but it would no doubt have been the focal point for some kind of ceremonial and religious customs.

In his *Rambles in Galloway* (1876), Malcolm MacLachlan Harper noted that:

> The circle consists of nineteen stones, with three in the centre standing in a line from east to west. They are all of unpolished granite, and the largest of the three in the centre is five and a half feet in diameter ... The stones on the circumference are from two to five feet long and from five to nearly twelve feet asunder, forming a circle of 218 feet.

The diameter of the whole monument measures over 60 feet. It is noticeable that the stones in the south-east quarter of the ring are slightly larger and of marginally greater height than those which form the remainder of the circle's perimeter.

In 1684, the Revd Andrew Symson, a seventeenth-century minister of nearby Kirkinner, wrote that the three large stones in the middle of the circle were called King Galdus's Tomb, thus fuelling further speculation that this was the burial place of the Scottish king. Whatever his actual place in history, it is far from certain that Galdus's remains lie at Torhouse anyway, as he is also thought to be entombed at Cairnholy II in Kirkdale. As well as being in an excellent state of preservation, the Torhouse Stone Circle is of interest due to its location; circles of this kind are normally to be found in north-east rather than south-west Scotland.

ST NINIAN'S CAVE

A POPULAR PLACE OF PILGRIMAGE ON THE GALLOWAY COAST

St Ninian's Cave lies on the coast approximately three miles south-west of Whithorn, where it appears as a distinctive fissure, cut deep into the cliffs along the pebble-strewn shoreline of Port Castle Bay. It can be easily identified by the array of votive offerings – many of which are pebbles taken from the beach and inscribed, by hand, with a cross – that have been left by visitors at the entrance to and also inside this popular place of pilgrimage.

St Ninian's Cave.

St Ninian is regarded as Scotland's first Christian saint, but very little is known about his life. Some sources suggest that he was born close to the Solway and later went off to study in Rome, where he was made a bishop by the Pope before arriving back in Scotland a few years later, around 397.

We catch a glimpse of him in the Venerable Bede's *Ecclesiastical History of the English People* (*c.* 730), where he is referred to as 'Bishop Ninias, a most reverent and holy man of the British nation, who had been regularly instructed at Rome in the faith and mysteries of the truth.'

One theory suggests that the cave stands close to the spot where St Ninian landed back on Scottish soil after his travels, and that he used it as a place for contemplation and solitude. Christopher N. Johnston reported in the 'Proceedings of the Society of Antiquaries of Scotland' in 1883 that,

Votive offerings at the entrance to St Ninian's Cave.

> Until recent years there was nothing except the name of the cave, and a vague tradition current in the district, to suggest that it had ever afforded shelter to a worthier guest than the rock pigeon. But the tradition which ascribed ecclesiastical associations to the place received a few years ago singular confirmation, by the discovery of a small cross carved upon the rock a few yards in front of the cave.

Further crosses were unearthed at the site and on the floor of the cave, and others had been discovered on the walls at an earlier date. Given that St Ninian had built a church at nearby Whithorn and had connections with the area, it is not unreasonable to assume, as Johnston concluded, that 'this cleft in the jagged rocks which now bears his name was associated with the life's work of the great saint of Galloway.'

THE CAVES OF KILHERN

NEOLITHIC BURIAL SITE NEAR NEW LUCE

Situated on a mound in open moorland, the Caves of Kilhern, although perhaps lacking the distinctive appearance of Cairnholy (see p. 34), are prehistoric remains well worthy of our attention. However, despite the name, these are not caves at all but a Neolithic chambered burial cairn dating from around 2,000-3,000 BC. Lying in the shadows of the giant wind turbines which have been erected on nearby Artfield Fell, there could hardly be a more striking juxtaposition of ancient and modern landscape features; a contrast rendered even starker by the remoteness of this lonely spot.

Sadly, the Caves of Kilhern have not fared well over the years. From the beginning of the eighteenth century, land was increasingly enclosed and stone walls were erected to form boundaries, and any suitable material found lying close at hand was used for the purpose. During this time, the Caves of Kilhern were much disturbed and robbed, as was the fate of many similar antiquities

A well preserved example of the Caves of Kilhern.

and, as a result, little of the communal Neolithic burial site survives intact. Most of the burial chambers lie open to the elements, except for one which still retains its cap, or cover stone. One antiquarian, writing at the end of the nineteenth century, suggested that a large stone (almost 7 feet long) from the Caves of Kilhern had found its way into a kitchen floor in New Luce.

THE MULL OF GALLOWAY
THE MOST SOUTHERLY POINT IN SCOTLAND

There is no doubt that the Mull of Galloway is the most southerly point in Scotland. Consult a map of Britain and you will find that it actually lies south of Penrith, Bishop Auckland and Hartlepool in England. Travelling south for twenty miles or so from the ferry port of Stranraer, through Ardwell and Drummore (which claims the distinction of being Scotland's most southerly village), it can seem a remote and isolated place as you approach ever nearer, along progressively minor roads, to the tip of the peninsula. The impression is greatly magnified when the landscape is drenched with horizontal rain and lashed by south-westerly gales. On a fine and clear day, however, the views across to Ireland and the Isle of Man are magnificent.

Gallie Craig at the Mull of Galloway, Scotland's most southerly point.

You know that you have almost reached your journey's end when the lighthouse comes into view. Known as Stevenson Tower, it was built by Robert Stevenson, a prominent member of the famous Scottish lighthouse-building family. (He was also the grandfather of author Robert Louis Stevenson.) Construction work on the lighthouse took two years to complete, and it finally came into operation in 1830. The lighthouse, owned and maintained by the Northern Lighthouse Board, was manned until 1988 but, like all Scottish – indeed UK – lighthouses, it is now automatic. In April 2005, the European Region Development Fund financed the installation of a webcam.

There is a small Royal Society for the Protection of Birds reserve at the Mull of Galloway (one of the smallest RSPB reserves in the country) which, not surprisingly, given the abundance of cliffs and rocky coastline, is a haven for seabirds, including fulmars, razorbills and guillemots all jostling for space on the narrow ledges in spring, with eider ducks and shags becoming a feature in the winter months. Summer brings gannets and pied wagtails, while in autumn, sand and house martins congregate prior to their migration to warmer climes.

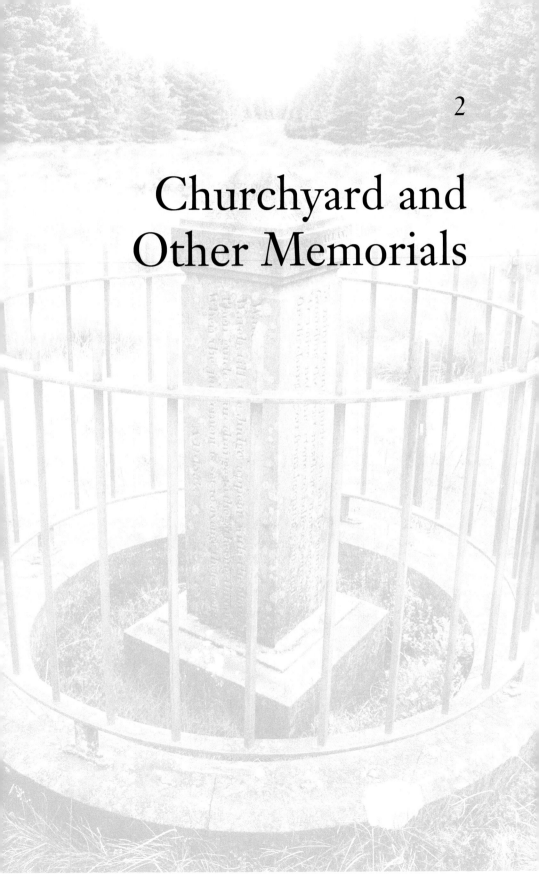

2

Churchyard and Other Memorials

THE MACDIARMID MEMORIAL
AN OPEN BOOK IN THE HILLS

The unusual Hugh MacDiarmid Memorial has the appearance of a giant open book perched on an exposed hillside high above Langholm, and that is precisely what the bronze and steel structure is supposed to represent. Dedicated to the memory of the Langholm-born poet and critic, the right- and left-hand 'pages' are crammed with images, including a whisky glass, pipe, birds, hills, the diagonal cross of the saltire and, above all, perhaps, a thistle; all of which are drawn from MacDiarmid's life and work.

Born in 1892 and the son of a postman, MacDiarmid (pen name Christopher Murray Grieve) became a journalist after leaving school, and later, in 1928, he helped found the National Party of Scotland, by which time he had become a leading figure in the Scottish literary renaissance of the twentieth century. Having at first published a quantity of poetry in English, he turned increasingly to a variant of the Scots language known as 'Lallans'. He wrote prolifically for half a century until his death in 1978, and gained a worldwide reputation.

The MacDiarmid Memorial above Langholm.

A detail from the memorial.

His major and lengthy work, *A Drunk Man Looks at the Thistle* (1926) is regarded as one of the great contributions to Scottish literature in the last century.

Executed by Jake Harvey and unveiled in August 1985, the eye-catching MacDiarmid Memorial was accomplished with support from – among many other sources – the Scottish Sculpture Trust and the Scottish Arts Council, together with Langholm Community Council and the Langholm MacDiarmid Committee. There is an echo of MacDiarmid's personality in the memorial's sharp corners, because he could certainly be irascible and he courted controversy. (For proof of this, you need look no further than his 'Who's Who' entry, where he gave 'Anglophobia' as his hobby.) However, he did possess a sense of humour too;

as the Communist Party candidate for the Kinross and West Perthshire constituency in the 1964 General Election, he garnered only 127 votes and lost to the winner by a margin of over 16,000 votes. He asked for a recount, because he couldn't believe that so many people had voted for him!

THOMAS CARLYLE: THE 'SAGE OF CHELSEA'
ECCLEFECHAN'S FAMOUS MAN OF LETTERS

Anyone familiar with the Thames Embankment in London could almost be forgiven for thinking that a small slice of Chelsea had been set down on the Haggs, in the Annandale village of Ecclefechan, 6 miles south of Lockerbie. In 1927, a large statue depicting the seated figure of the philosopher and historian, Thomas Carlyle, was placed at the top of the hill leading down into the village from the north. The statue is a replica of the figure created in the 1870s by sculptor Sir Joseph Boehm, and erected between Cheyne Row and the Albert Embankment. The son of a stonemason, Thomas Carlyle was born in 1775 at the distinctive Arched House in Ecclefechan; a house that had been built only a few years earlier by his father and an uncle (also a stonemason).

In 1809, at the age of fourteen, Carlyle left his native village and walked the eighty miles or so north to Edinburgh,

Carlyle's statue at Ecclefechan.

The Arched House that was Carlyle's birthplace.

where he took up his place at the university. After toying with careers in teaching, the Church and the law, he eventually left Edinburgh without taking his degree and, over the years that followed, became one of the nineteenth century's most famous and distinguished men of letters. His principal works included a three-volume *History of the French Revolution* (1837), *The Life and Letters of Oliver Cromwell* (1845), and the monumental six-volume biography *Frederick the Great* (1858-65), which took him fourteen years to complete and which, in his *Reminiscences*, he described himself 'wrestling with … as with the ugliest dragon which blotted out all the daylight and the rest of the world to me, till I should get it slain.' By the time of his death in 1881 at No. 24 Cheyne Row, (where he had lived for almost fifty years), Carlyle had become affectionately known as the 'Sage of Chelsea'.

Despite his international celebrity, Carlyle never forgot – or sought to conceal – his humble origins. His friend and biographer J.A. Froude wrote that he was buried in Ecclefechan churchyard 'as he was born, as he lived, an Annandale peasant'. Even in death, Carlyle's impressive figure presides over the village of his birth.

'OLD MORTALITY'

THE ITINERANT LIFE OF ROBERT PATERSON, STONEMASON

Apart from an unobtrusively carved hammer and chisel set above the inscription, the gravestone of Robert Paterson in Caerlaverock parish churchyard at Bankend has no obvious distinguishing features. However, closer inspection reveals that this red sandstone memorial marks the final resting place of the 'Old Mortality' of Sir Walter Scott, who was buried here in February 1801. The gravestone was erected in 1869 by Scott's publisher, many years after Paterson's death at Caerlaverock. The connection between Paterson, a stonemason by trade, and the world-famous author was an unlikely one, but it was cemented through the novel that Scott published in 1816 (as part of his *Tales of My Landlord* series), whose title bears Paterson's nickname of 'Old Mortality'.

The gravestone of 'Old Mortality' in Caerlaverock churchyard.

Paterson, who was born in 1715 near Hawick, left his home and family at

Memorial to 'Old Mortality' at Balmaclellan.

Gatelawbridge near Thornhill in 1745 and travelled mainly through south-west Scotland, refurbishing, cutting and erecting gravestones to the memory of those Covenanters who had perished during the Killing Times of the late-seventeenth century. 'Whether family dissensions, or the deep and enthusiastic feeling of supposed duty, drove him to leave his dwelling and adopt the singular mode of life in which he wandered … through Scotland, is not known,' reflected Scott in his introduction to *Old Mortality*. 'It could not be poverty, however, which prompted his journeys, for he never accepted anything beyond the hospitality which was willingly rendered him, and when that was not proffered, he always had money enough to provide for his own humble wants.'

Scott met Paterson in person on one of 'Old Mortality's' rare jaunts north, in the churchyard at Dunnottar near Stonehaven. He drew on the occasion for his description of the stonemason's personal appearance in the novel:

A blue bonnet of unusual dimensions covered the grey hairs of the pious workman. His dress was a large old-fashioned coat of the coarse cloth called hoddingrey … with waistcoat and breeches of the same. Although I had never seen the old man before, yet from the singularity of his employment and the style of his equipage, I had no difficulty in recognizing a religious itinerant whom I had often heard talked of, and who was known in various parts of Scotland by the title of 'Old Mortality'.

CHOLERA IN DUMFRIES

A DISEASE TAMED BY CLEAN RUNNING WATER

The large memorial tablet presiding over the Cholera Mound in St Michael's churchyard in Dumfries is a permanent reminder of just how great a scourge the disease once was, in the days before supplies of clean running water and proper sanitation arrangements in general. Whenever the pestilence visited a village, town or city, it spread rapidly through the population and decimated it. Dumfries was no exception and, in 1832, the town was ripe for an outbreak, as local historian William McDowall recounted:

> With the exception of what was furnished by a few wells and private pumps all the water used for domestic purposes was carried by hand or carted in barrels from the Nith, by four old men, who doled it out in tin pitchers or cans, from door to door at the rate of five canfuls a penny. The river, when swelled by heavy rains, which was often the case, became thick with mud; and it was constantly exposed to a more noxious pollution, caused by the refuse poured into it from the town.

The memorial on the Cholera Mound, where most of the victims were buried, records that 420 inhabitants of Dumfries (from a population of about 12,000), died from the disease in the period between 15 September and 27 November 1832, and that at least 900 people were infected. (Of course, it should be remembered that these statistics exclude Maxwelltown, which was a separate

Cholera memorial in St Michael's churchyard, Dumfries.

Water fountain in High Street, Dumfries. It was erected to celebrate the introduction of piped water to the town.

burgh at that time). Cholera visited Dumfries again in 1848, when its effects were almost as severe as the 1832 outbreak.

However, three years after this second epidemic, and hastened on by these twin disasters, a gravitational water supply was at last introduced to Dumfries, piped from Lochrutton Loch (four miles west of the town), and a fountain was erected in the High Street to celebrate the event. The original was replaced in 1882 by the present ornate confection of stone and cast-iron bowls, with jets of water being channelled through the mouths of dolphins and crocodiles.

DEATH NEAR THE DEVIL'S BEEF TUB

A MEMORIAL TO TWO BRAVE POSTMEN

On 1 February 1831, in the late afternoon as darkness fell, two postmen – driver John Goodfellow and guard James MacGeorge – guided their mail coach out of Moffat during a raging snowstorm, bound for Edinburgh. The route was an arduous one at the best of times but, as events would prove, impossible in such atrocious conditions. Despite being hauled by a team of six horses, the vehicle became stuck in a snowdrift two miles beyond Moffat. Leaving four of the horses with a local road mender, Goodfellow and MacGeorge set out with the remaining two horses, intent on continuing their journey to the next stage along the route – the inn at Tweedshaws, which was five miles

Cairn built in memory of the two postmen who perished in the snow.

away. Their progress must have been desperately slow as they followed the steep and exposed road up Ericstane Brae in driving snow. After about three miles, and unable to make any further headway in the blizzard, the horses were abandoned. (They turned up later, safe but rider-less, at a nearby farm.)

Meanwhile, it seems that Goodfellow and MacGeorge had divided the heavy mailbags between them and continued on foot in the darkness along the remote road that skirted the summit of the Devil's Beef Tub. At the sixth snow post – placed at intervals along the route to guide travellers in bad weather conditions – from Moffat they relinquished their burdens, tying the necks of the mailbags around the post for safekeeping. Four days later a search party found their bodies in the snow; only the tips of Goodfellow's boots were visible in a deep drift, but MacGeorge, although half-buried, was in a kneeling position. It is thought that he died where he landed from falling through sheer exhaustion.

In 1931, to mark the 100th anniversary of the tragic event, a simple cairn built of native whinstone, and bearing a carved replica of the guard's bugle, was placed by the roadside at the site of the sixth snow post, where it can be seen today; a permanent reminder of the courage and devotion to duty displayed by two brave postmen.

'JEANIE DEANS'

THE STORY OF HELEN WALKER

Visitors to Irongray churchyard, a few miles north-west of Dumfries, may be puzzled to see an otherwise unremarkable tombstone surrounded by tall railings. On closer inspection they will find that it is the grave of local spinster Helen Walker, who died in 1791 aged eighty. For years she had eked out a meagre living by rearing chickens and working in the fields, but there lurked an incident in her far-distant past that was eventually to transform her from plain Helen Walker into 'Jeanie Deans', the heroine of Sir Walter Scott's novel *The Heart of Midlothian* (1818).

Helen Walker was twenty-seven when, in 1738, her younger sister Isobel was found guilty of child murder at the High Court in Dumfries. Isobel had given birth to a stillborn daughter and placed the body in the Cluden Water which ran close by the Walkers' cottage. Isobel's conviction arose from the fact that she had concealed both her pregnancy and the child's birth from everyone she knew, and then pleaded ignorance of an infant's body found in the river around the same time. The case was a harrowing one indeed. The defence counsel believed that if Helen would testify that her sister had told her about the infant's birth, then Isobel would be released. Helen refused to testify falsely, and Isobel was sentenced to death.

However, Helen set off immediately on foot to London, where she proved successful in obtaining a Royal Pardon for her sister. By the time she arrived back in Dumfries a month later, she had walked 700 miles.

Subsequently, Sir Walter Scott came to hear of these events, and he was so affected by Helen's epic journey and its purpose, that he wove a similar incident into the plot of *The Heart of Midlothian*. Helen became 'Jeanie Deans', Scott's personal favourite among all the heroines he created; 'The lass kept tugging at my heart,' he said.

In 1831, Scott paid for a memorial to be placed on Helen's grave, and he wrote the words that can still be read on the tombstone today. Over the ensuing years, as Helen Walker's connection with 'Jeanie Deans' became more widely known, souvenir hunters damaged the memorial to such an extent that it became necessary to place iron railings around it for protection.

The grave of 'Jeanie Deans' in Irongray churchyard.

THE QUEENSBERRY MARBLES
AN IMPRESSIVE EIGHTEENTH-CENTURY MARBLE CONFECTION

Those who find grandiose romantic gestures appealing need look no further than the parish church at Durisdeer, in remote Upper Nithsdale; 'perhaps one of the prettiest country churches to be seen in Scotland', according to a local eighteenth-century minister, the Revd Peter Rae. Here, adjoining the present building which was completed in 1720, a separate black-and-white marble aisle, which was formerly attached to an earlier church on the site, houses the famous Queensberry Marbles. Although it is possible to see this huge baroque monument through a window from the main body of the church itself, a door at the rear of the building allows direct access to the Queensberry Aisle, with its family burial chamber beneath.

The marble memorial was the work of the Flemish sculptor John van Nost and dates from 1713, a few years before the earlier medieval church at Durisdeer was demolished. It was erected to the memory of James, the Second Duke of Queensberry, who died in 1711, and his Duchess, Mary, who predeceased him in 1709. The couple are shown in a suitably romantic posture, with the husband gazing down adoringly at his recumbent wife, against a background of cherubs and Corinthian columns. The Second Duke had been created a Knight of the Garter in 1701, and it is in his Garter Robes that he is shown here.

The Queensberry Marbles in Durisdeer parish church.

The fulsome inscription tells its own story:

To Mary, Duchess of Queensberry and Dover, who being sprung on the father's side from the very illustrious families of Burlington and Cumberland, and on the mother's side from those of Somerset and Essex, tempered the splendour of her lineage by a winning disposition, heightened by its greatness of spirit and rendered, by the seductive allurement of her wit and beauty, her sterner nature pleasing and acceptable to her most loving husband [who] has caused this monument to be erected with this hope and only solace, that under the same tomb, where he has placed these beloved ashes, he will place his own …

His wish was, of course, duly granted, although somewhat sooner perhaps than he might have desired, given that he was still only forty-eight when he died.

COVENANTING MARTYRS
RELIGIOUS PERSECUTION IN THE KILLING TIMES

Put simply, Covenanters were people who, in the seventeenth century, refused to accept or acknowledge the monarch as the head of the Presbyterian Church, asserting that only Jesus Christ could occupy that position. Those individuals who could not accept the Stuart King, Charles I, as their spiritual leader, in 1638 signed the National Covenant to that effect. As a result they – and successive generations – endured years of persecution, and many people sacrificed their lives for the position they held. This terrible period came to be known as the Killing Times.

Fearing for their safety, Covenanters were forced to meet in secluded and often remote places to worship in secret, always with the knowledge that, should they be discovered by the soldiers whose job it was to seek them out, then imprisonment, transportation or, far more likely, death would surely follow.

One such popular meeting place was Whigs' Hole, a large hollow near the top of Altry Hill, where a hundred or so people could be accommodated without being seen. The sandstone pillar known as Allan's Cairn, which stands nearby on a remote stretch of the Southern Upland Way, indicates what happened after one such open-air service (or conventicle) had been held. The Covenanters were discovered by a troop of dragoons who pursued them across open country. George Allan and Margaret Gracie were captured and shot near the Fawns of Altry. They were later buried by friends at the spot marked by this monument. The present cairn, which was erected in 1857, replaces an earlier one.

At Kippford, a wooden stake, which can be found on the banks of the Urr Estuary, marks the spot where eighteen-year-old Margaret Wilson perished. Like many other Covenanters who suffered the same fate, she was callously

Wooden stake at Kippford.

Remote Allan's Cairn, on the Southern Upland Way.

tied to a stake and simply left to drown. It is said that as the Solway tide came in and gradually closed over her she sang the twenty-fifth Psalm, and that as she died 'her auburn hair was last seen floating as a symbol of her defiance and a warning to others.'

CHURCHYARD FURNITURE

INTERESTING DISCOVERIES AT SANQUHAR, TUNDERGARTH AND NEW GALLOWAY

Churchyards can produce very satisfying results for seekers of the strange or unusual. At Sanquhar, for example, telling their own obviously poignant but now long-forgotten story, lie two adjacent coffin-shaped tombstones. One is much larger than the other, and they commemorate the deaths of Rachel Hair and her child, who were killed by Cromwell's soldiers in 1657.

At rural Tundergarth, a few miles east of Lockerbie, there are several items of interest. One headstone, lying half-hidden among the encroaching vegetation and dating from the mid-eighteenth century, was erected to the memory of a local stonemason, George McLean, and bears a charming full-length carving of his portrait. Elsewhere, among the more conventional headstones and memorials in

The tombstones of Rachel Hair and her child at Sanquhar.

George McLean's headstone at Tundergarth.

this isolated churchyard, are a scattering of headstones which, bearing death masks and skulls and crossbones, provide stark and startling representations and reminders of death.

At Kells churchyard in New Galloway, the visitor will discover a fair example of an early eighteenth-century 'Adam and Eve' stone, showing the biblical pair on either side of the Tree of Knowledge in the Garden of Eden. A headstone dating from 1777 commemorates John Murray, who served as a local gamekeeper for almost half a century. It depicts some of the tools of his trade, including a dog, grouse and gun. An inscription carved on the reverse side reads:

John Murray's headstone at Kells churchyard, New Galloway.

Ah John, what changes since I saw thee last;
Thy fishing and thy shooting days are past,
Bagpipes and hautboys thou canst sound no more,
Thy nods, grimaces, winks and pranks are o'er.
Thy joys on earth
A snuff, a glass, riddles and noisy mirth,
Are vanished all. Yet blest, I hope thou art
For in thy station weel thou playdst thy part.

UNUSUAL MEMORIALS IN BALMACLELLAN CHURCHYARD

SCOTLAND'S FIRST CIVIC WAR MEMORIAL AND A WITCH'S GRAVE

The churchyard at Balmaclellan contains two particularly unusual memorials. The first of the pair – a large red sandstone pillar erected around 1856 – commemorates five local men who died during the Crimean War of 1853-56. A sixth local casualty, who died at Sebastopol in 1855, is remembered by a separate nearby gravestone. Erected in the churchyard by

Crimean War memorial in Balmaclellan churchyard, with its cannon decoration at the top.

the people of the village, the pillar is the first documented civic war memorial in Scotland. It also lays claim to being the country's only civic memorial dedicated to those who served and perished in the Crimean War. In addition to bearing an inscription giving details of the local men who fell, the pillar is decorated with carvings depicting some of the paraphernalia of nineteenth-century warfare, including a cannon and cannonballs, a pair of crossed swords and a rifle.

Elsewhere, perched on the steeply-raked western boundary of the churchyard, a roughly-hewn pillar of stone, which bears no inscription and is thought to have been placed there in the mid-nineteenth century among the more conventional headstones of that period, is believed to mark the grave of Elspeth McEwen, who has the unenviable distinction of being the last witch to be executed in southern Scotland. She was burned alive at the stake on a hill at Kirkcudbright, on 24 August 1698.

Witch-hunts were an ever-present scourge of seventeenth-century Scotland (and elsewhere), and no mercy was shown to those poor women who were found guilty of dabbling in the black arts, no matter how slender the evidence against them or how unreliable the testimony. The accusations levelled at Elspeth McEwen, who lived in Balmaclellan parish, revolved around her alleged bewitching of her neighbours' hens and cattle. Her situation was not improved by claims that she was able to transform herself into the shape of a hare, nor by the fact that, as Sir Herbert Maxwell wrote in his *History of Dumfries and Galloway* (1900), 'The minister's horse, which was sent to bring her up for trial, trembled with fear when

This stone in Balmaclellan churchyard is believed to mark the grave of Elspeth McEwen.

she mounted, and sweated drops of blood.' One truly chilling fact to emerge from a record of the whole barbaric affair, was that the executioner employed to dispatch Elspeth McEwen was supplied – as a part of his remuneration – with a pint of ale to quench his thirst while she was burning.

BILLY MARSHALL'S GRAVE
THE LAST RESTING PLACE OF A 'GYPSY KING'

Seeking out a particular gravestone in sprawling St Cuthbert's churchyard, Kirkcudbright, is like searching for the proverbial needle in a haystack. However, owing to its recent renovation, Billy Marshall's headstone – with its bold inscription on the front, coupled with the distinctive crossed spoons and ram's horns motif on the back – is not too hard to locate (despite being only about 2½ feet square).

Billy Marshall was the renowned 'King of the Gypsies', who reputedly died at the advanced age of 120 in 1792. Marshall was a bandit and smuggler, a maker of horn spoons and cups (hence the decoration on his gravestone), who led and ruled his people for more than eighty years. He was born into a renowned gypsy family and was married at least seventeen times. As a young man, he is said to have fought at the Battle of the Boyne in King William's army, and later served

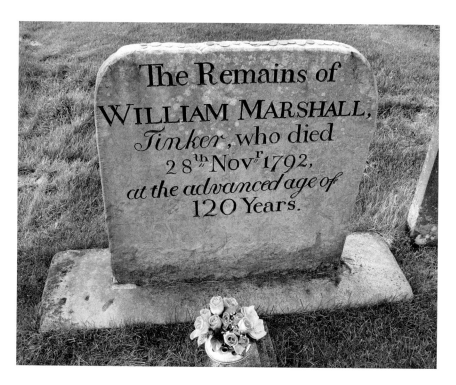

Above & below: *The front and back of Billy Marshall's grave in St Cuthbert's churchyard, Kirkcudbright.*

under the 1st Duke of Marlborough. Precisely when he acquired his title of 'King of the Gypsies' in the south-west (and whether he achieved this status without bloodshed) is unclear, but he was certainly still a young man at the time.

Marshall was obviously a strong and charismatic personality, and not someone to be trifled with. Writing in his *Exploits and Anecdotes of the Scottish Gypsies* (1821), William Chambers described how 'after Billy was firmly seated on the throne of his predecessor he made a progress over his extensive dominions, with the intention to punish severely those neighbouring gypsy chiefs who had made invasions on his empire.'

According to Chambers, Marshall, who 'practised every crime which is incident to human nature [including] those of the deepest dye,' has, to this day, certainly retained the legendary status that he acquired during his lifetime. His gravestone remains a magnet for visitors from all over the world, and coins are often placed on it as offerings. It is also a lodestone for travellers, many of whom, it is said, visit during the hours of darkness. In 1992, on the morning following the 200th anniversary of Marshall's death, his gravestone, which had been all but bare the previous evening, was apparently decorated with flowers and heaped with coins, suggesting there had been many nocturnal visitors on that special occasion.

SEAFARING REMINDERS IN KIRKCUDBRIGHT
A SCULPTURE, A WEATHERVANE AND A STREET LAMP

Long before it became a magnet for artists during the nineteenth century, Kirkcudbright was a thriving port with a bustling harbour, situated at the mouth of the River Dee. Sadly, the town's fortunes seem to have been in the doldrums when Daniel Defoe passed through while writing his monumental *Tour thro the Whole Island of Great Britain* (1724-6). 'Here is a harbour without ships,' he recorded, 'a port without trade, a fishery without nets, a people without business.' As downbeat assessments go, it was pretty emphatic. However, just over a century later, the New Statistical Account of 1843 was able to report that 'Twenty-six vessels belong to the port … [and] in 1840, the Custom House port of Kirkcudbright, with its creeks, possesses fifty-four vessels.'

The Harbour Sculpture on Fisherman's Green.

There is probably not a port in the land whose people have not experienced the loss of lives in tragedies at sea, and Kirkcudbright is no exception. The highly individual 'Harbour Sculpture', fashioned out of a green oak tree trunk by Charlie Easterfield, stands on the town's Fisherman's Green. Unveiled in 1994, and comprising a watchful mother and child gazing expectantly seawards, it serves as a memorial to those who have perished at sea.

Although not strictly related to the activities of the port, there are another couple of particularly interesting features to be seen with sea-going connections. High above the streets of Kirkcudbright, a weathervane with a distinctly nautical flavour rests atop the steeple of the Tolbooth. It is thought to have originally been placed there some time after 1805, to mark the Battle of Trafalgar, and serves as a popular perch for the bird population of Kirkcudbright.

Down below, at street level, a lamp standard bearing a stained-glass representation of St Cuthbert arriving at Kirkcudbright by sea can be found outside the Tolbooth. The seventh-century saint is thought to have visited here during his travels as a missionary. (The name of the town derives from the Church of St Cuthbert.) Two centuries after St Cuthbert's death at Lindisfarne in 687, the Northumbrian priory was abandoned following raids by the Vikings. The monks subsequently travelled from one place to another, carrying St Cuthbert's remains with them. His bones are thought to have rested at Kirkcudbright for some time during their travels.

Battle of Trafalgar weathervane on top of the Tolbooth steeple.

Lamp standard outside the Tolbooth.

THE GAVIN MAXWELL OTTER MEMORIAL

REFLECTIONS OF 'RING OF BRIGHT WATER' ON THE GALLOWAY COAST

A beautifully executed life-size figure of an otter, cast in bronze and sculpted by Penny Wheatley, could hardly be a more fitting memorial to the author and naturalist Gavin Maxwell. Standing high on a hillside, it overlooks the Point of Lag and Monreith Bay, near Maxwell's childhood home on the Galloway coast.

Born in 1914, Maxwell was the son of an aristocratic Lowland family. In his book, *The House of Elrig* (1965), he described his unusual early upbringing, spent largely among the wild and windswept Galloway moors. However, his name will probably always be more closely associated with his worldwide bestseller, *Ring of Bright Water* (1960), which charted the ups and downs of his life spent with otters at the remote spot on the West Highland coast that he christened 'Camusfearna', in order to preserve its anonymity (and which was, in fact, called Sandaig, situated five or so miles south of Glenelg). He continued the story of his unconventional household in two further books, *The Rocks Remain* (1963) and *Raven Seek Thy Brother* (1968).

The Gavin Maxwell Otter Memorial near Monreith.

The bronze figure – seeming so small in the wide landscape – has a vulnerable and ethereal quality about it, especially for those who are acquainted with Maxwell's somewhat tempestuous life and complex personality through the biographies that have been written about him; and for those who are familiar with the sad end that befell at least two of his beloved otters – Mij, killed at the hands of a local Highland road mender, and Edal, who perished in the house fire that brought Maxwell's life at 'Camusfearna' to an end. The siting of this unusual memorial is particularly appropriate, as Maxwell (who died in 1969) is said to have exercised his otters on the beach below this hillside when he returned to the area from his West Highland home.

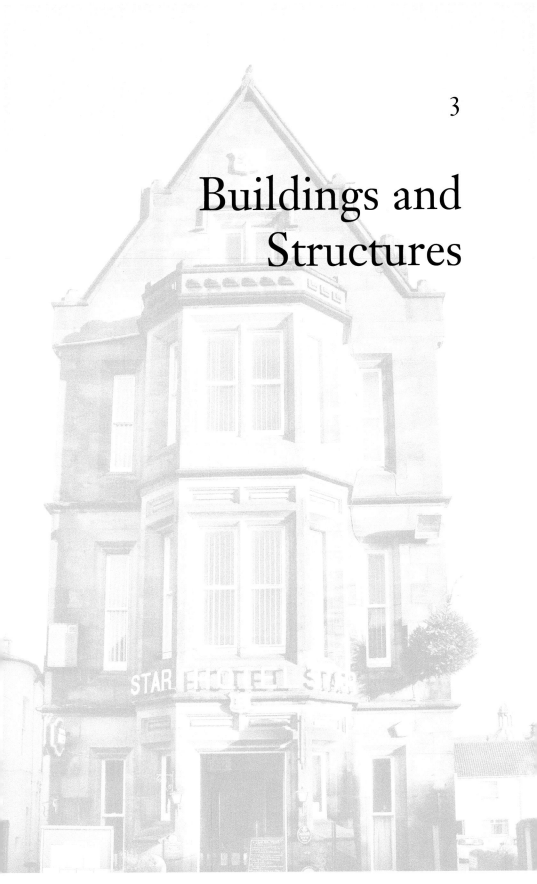

3

Buildings and Structures

KAGYU SAMYE LING

A TASTE OF TIBET IN ESKDALEMUIR

The large stupa (or pagoda).

The Liberation Gate.

A section of the prayer wheel house.

In a landscape enveloped in coniferous plantations, Eskdalemuir can sometimes have a gloomy air, especially when mist or low cloud clings doggedly to the treetops. Furthermore, regular followers of the television or radio weather forecast may recognise the name because Eskdalemuir seems to crop up with some regularity as either the coldest or wettest place in Britain. Nowadays, however, the truly distinguishing feature of Eskdalemuir lies in the presence of the Kagyu Samye Ling Monastery and Tibetan Buddhist Centre, which was founded in the valley (initially at Johnstone House) in 1967. It was the first major Tibetan centre to be established in the Western world. The centre has developed and markedly grown over the past forty-five years, but lying among woods and landscaped gardens it still manages not to impose itself on the Eskdalemuir landscape, while undeniably bringing a blaze of colour to the valley.

Even the main temple – the building that must be regarded as the hub of the centre – lies almost hidden from the road, except for tantalizing glimpses through the trees of its soaring pagoda roof. It was constructed over a number of years (by centre residents and visitors, and as money allowed) in traditional Tibetan style, and was officially opened on 8 August 1988 (supposedly the most propitious day of the decade). The main shrine room, situated on the ground floor of the temple, is open to visitors and residents alike.

The centre is a magnet for those drawn to Buddhist teachings, and provides opportunities for short and long-term retreats, while inevitably proving something of a tourist attraction as well. Indeed, there is much for the visitor to see in addition to the temple itself, including the prayer wheel house (each prayer wheel holds over thirty-two million mantras or short prayers); a large stupa (or pagoda) symbolising the enlightened mind of the Buddha; the Butterlamp House, dedicated to world peace; the Liberation Gate, which echoes the style of those entrances found in Tibetan monasteries, and statues of early influential Buddhist figures, such as Nagarjuna and Guru Rinpoche. In addition, the entire Centre is draped with streams of colourful prayer flags.

THE TOLL HOUSE GRETNA, AND GRETNA GREEN
FAVOURITE HAUNTS FOR RUNAWAY LOVERS

Gretna Green is famous throughout the world as the village to which couples in search of a hasty wedding fled. In England, during the mid-eighteenth century, the Marriage Act forbade any young couple, where one of the pair was under twenty-one years of age, to marry without parental consent. This law did not apply in Scotland, and so Gretna Green, being situated just over the border with England, became 'the resort of all amorous couples whose union the prudence of parents or guardians prohibits', according to Thomas Pennant, in his *Tour of Scotland in 1769*. 'Here the young pair may be instantly united by a fisherman, a joiner or a blacksmith.' There were several places in the village itself where such marriages

Above & below: *The old toll house and adjacent 'marriage room' in Gretna.*

were performed, but the toll house at Gretna, just under a mile south of Gretna Green and just over the bridge which crosses the River Sark (the 'first' or 'last' house in Scotland depending on the direction of your journey), became an obvious attraction. 'This is the first building over the border, and it is situated close thereunto,' declared Peter Orlando Hutchinson in his *Chronicles of Gretna Green* (1844). 'It is on the chief road of the country, over which everyone journeying into western Scotland must pass; in fine, it is there like the open mouth of a net set against the stream.' Within the space of six years alone, 1,300 couples were joined in matrimony in the 'marriage room' which stands next door to the toll house. A notice on the wall states that 10,000 weddings were performed in the building altogether.

In Jane Austen's *Pride and Prejudice* (1813), for example, Lydia Bennet writes to an acquaintance after she has eloped with George Wickham: 'You will laugh when you know where I am gone … I am going to Gretna Green, and if you cannot guess with who, I shall think you such a simpleton,' proving that Gretna Green became celebrated enough to enter the great literature of the age. However, Gretna Green ceased to prove such a magnet after 1857, when a law was passed requiring twenty-one days' residence in Scotland before a Scottish wedding could be performed.

THE 'DEVIL'S PORRIDGE'
HM FACTORY GRETNA: THE MUNITIONS PLANT THAT WASN'T ON THE MAP

The vast First World War cordite manufacturing plant, known as HM Factory Gretna, stretched for about ten miles from Longtown in Cumbria and along the northern edge of the Solway Firth to Dornock, near Annan. It was built in response to the ill-equipped British Army's urgent need for ammunition, with cordite being an essential explosive ingredient used in the shells and bullets that were sent out to the front line.

Although the munitions plant was built on an unprecedented scale, there was, for security reasons, no reference made to it on local Ordnance Survey maps. It was even given a codename – Moorside – to camouflage its existence. Eventually, more than 16,000 people (two-thirds of them women) were employed there, some of whom had been drawn from Britain's far-flung empire overseas, and the two townships of Gretna and Eastriggs were specially created to house them, in this hitherto sparsely populated area.

In 1916, during a visit to HM Factory Gretna, Sir Arthur Conan Doyle, the creator of *Sherlock Holmes*, coined the term 'Devil's Porridge', when he saw for himself the munitions workers mixing nitro-glycerine and nitro-cotton together into a form of dry explosive paste, which became the cordite or 'Devil's Porridge'.

'This is where the danger comes in,' he explained. 'The smallest generation of heat may cause an explosion. Those smiling khaki-clad girls who are swirling the stuff round in their hands would be blown to atoms in an instant if certain very small changes occurred.' At its height, HM Factory Gretna produced a staggering 800 tons of cordite each week.

A private railway system threaded its way between the various sites that comprised this huge industrial complex. Reminders of it can still be found, such as the derelict railway bridge at either side of the River Sark on the now dismantled stretch of line that ran just south of Gretna. Also, the railway engine that resides outside the building which now houses the 'Devil's Porridge' exhibition in Eastriggs, formerly pulled the carriages that carried the paste from the Dornock site to the Mossband site. It is one of only a couple of such engines still remaining that were associated with the munitions factory.

A derelict bridge on HM Factory Gretna's former private railway line.

A rare surviving example of one of HM Factory Gretna's railway engines.

HM Factory Gretna closed down at the end of the First World War and the plant was demolished. However, Gretna and Eastriggs continue to be thriving communities.

THE SOLWAY VIADUCT

A BRAVE ATTEMPT TO CROSS THE SOLWAY BY RAIL

The course of the old railway line that once ran south from Annan to Seafield can still be clearly seen. In fact, a section of the former trackbed has been put to good use in recent years, as it now forms a part of the Annan Shore Walk. At Seafield, a viaduct carried the line across the Solway Firth to Bowness-on-Solway on the English side where, at Herdhill Scar, a fragment of the original wrought- and cast-iron structure can still be seen.

Designed by the Kelso-born civil engineer Sir James Brunlees, the Solway Viaduct was opened in 1869 and was just over a mile in length. By providing a link between Brayton, on the Maryport and Carlisle Railway, and the Caledonian Railway, near Kirtlebridge, the Solway Junction Railway (of which the viaduct formed a crucial part) enabled iron-ore to be transported via a 'short-cut' from the mines of West Cumberland to the steelworks in Lanarkshire, without having to travel through Carlisle. In 1870, the line began carrying passengers as well.

The history of the Solway Viaduct proved to be a chequered and fairly brief one. An uneasy relationship quickly developed between the natural forces of the Solway Firth and the man-made viaduct, with the situation reaching a crisis early in 1881. Following a particularly hard winter, large sheets of ice melted in the river, and the power exerted by the strengthening tide on the pillars of the structure caused the viaduct to collapse in two places. Repairs were made and the viaduct was reopened three years later.

Following the outbreak of the First World War, rail traffic across the Solway Viaduct appears to have ceased or, at best, became extremely limited. When the war ended four years later, the structure was in need of considerable renovation, and it was eventually closed to all rail services in 1921. However, it

The course of the former trackbed at Seafield, from where the railway line crossed over to England on the Solway Viaduct.

took a further thirteen years before the viaduct was finally dismantled; a delay that proved to be a boon in some quarters. In those days, when the English licensing laws were more relaxed than those on the Scottish side, it apparently became a familiar sight on Sundays to see men crossing the disused viaduct on foot, in search of their daily pint.

THE ANNANDALE DISTILLERY
'A LITTLE GEM OF SCOTLAND'S INDUSTRIAL HISTORY'

The Annandale Distillery at Northfield, Annan, lay out on the Warmanbie road a mile or so north of the town and fragments of the original building can still be seen there.

In 1814, the dramatist Richard Ayton noted that 'from the prevalence of red noses' he had observed when passing through Annan, whisky was clearly the inhabitants' favourite drink. However, a further sixteen years were to elapse before George Donald, an excise officer, started the Annandale Distillery in 1830. Half a century later, the reins were taken over by John Gardner, who installed a new plant to bring the distilling process up to date. When Alfred Barnard visited the premises during the 1880s, while researching his definitive book *Whisky Distilleries of the United Kingdom*, the yearly output of pure malt was in the region of 28,000 gallons. However, despite making many improvements – replacing the old waterwheel with a turbine, for example, and introducing steam power – Gardner's stay at Northfield was comparatively brief, and in the early 1890s the distillery was taken over by John Walker & Sons Ltd.

Whisky has not been produced at Northfield since 1919 and, once all the stock had been disposed of, the Annandale Distillery site reverted to simply being a farm again. When Barnard had paid his visit over thirty years earlier, he had noted how the distillery itself stood cheek by jowl with 'quite a model farmstead; the cowsheds, piggeries and stables being ranged round the square yard. We saw upwards of twenty-five head of cattle almost ready for the butcher, and a considerable number of pigs, all fed from the draff or grains from the distillery.'

(Note: At the time of writing, the fortunes of the Annandale Distillery – once described as 'a little gem of Scotland's industrial history' – are about to be revived, with rebuilding work in progress.)

An original chimney at the old Annandale Distillery.

REPENTANCE TOWER ON TRAILTROW HILL
A SIXTEENTH-CENTURY WATCHTOWER WITH SAD UNDERTONES

Repentance Tower on Trailtrow Hill.

It is quite a steep walk up to Repentance Tower in its graveyard setting at the top of Trailtrow Hill, Hoddom, but the panoramic views alone make the effort worthwhile. The Solway Firth and the Cumbrian fells are spread out to the south; while the Lowther and Tweedsmuir Hills are to the north. Its height and position made Trailtrow Hill the perfect spot on which to build a watchtower – one in a line of such Border beacons designed to warn of invasions from the south.

The origins of the tower itself and, in particular, how it acquired its unusual name, are somewhat hazy. Built sometime in the mid-sixteenth century by Lord Herries (Sir John Maxwell of Terregles before his marriage to Agnes Herries), the word 'Repentence' [*sic*] is carved into the lintel above the front door of the sandstone tower. Various stories have attached themselves over the years to this unusual and poignant inscription, although one version in particular is felt to carry more weight than any other.

Prior to his ennoblement through marriage, the aforementioned John Maxwell had apparently been obliged to 'pledge his allegiance' to England, after Dumfriesshire had been taken by the English in one of the Border skirmishes (a regular feature of life at that time). His decision to fight against the English in a subsequent battle led to the execution of fourteen of his countrymen at Carlisle, who had been taken hostage as a guarantee of Maxwell's good faith. It is thought possible that Lord Herries subsequently built a watchtower on this exposed spot (reputedly using stones from the nearby Trailtrow Chapel) as a monument to the men who had perished as a result of his change of heart, and that the name of the tower perhaps echoed his regret at their deaths.

UKRANIAN PRISONER-OF-WAR CHAPEL, HALLMUIR
'EVOCATIVE REMINDER OF WARTIME SPIRIT'

The Ukranian Prisoner-of-War Chapel at Hallmuir, near Lockerbie, is one particular example of how the indomitable nature of the human spirit can shine. During the Second World War, the camp at Hallmuir housed

German and Italian prisoners. In 1947 it became 'home' to approximately 450 Ukranians, who had previously been British-held prisoners-of-war in Italy – men who had been coerced into fighting on the German side against Russia, and who would otherwise suffer serious reprisals against their own families and homes in the Ukraine. At the end of the war, when they were mistakenly viewed as traitors, the men were unable to go home without fearing for

The Ukranian Prisoner-of-War Chapel at Hallmuir.

their lives. As a result, several thousand Ukranians came to Britain classed as 'surrendered enemy personnel'. The men who arrived at Hallmuir were directed by the Ministry of Agriculture to work on local farms and in forestry.

Model of Kiev Cathedral, hand-carved using a penknife.

The camp at Hallmuir comprised about forty single-storey huts made of corrugated iron, and Sir John Buchanan Jardine (who owned the land) allocated one of these buildings to be used as a church for the prisoners-of-war.

At first, the inside of the hut was simple and unadorned but, over the course of time and with incredible patience, imagination and skill, the men transformed the interior, with its panoply of hand-crafted objects, into what can still be seen in all its glory today. For example, there are candlesticks made from old shell casings, hand-painted religious pictures, a large and colourful chandelier fashioned out of old coat hangers and fencing wire, and, perhaps most impressive of all, a splendidly detailed model of the bombed Kiev Cathedral, carved by hand using a simple penknife. A letter from Historic Scotland, dated December 2003, which is displayed in the chapel comments that the building is an 'evocative reminder of wartime spirit, and the way the prisoners found ways to overcome the privations of their situation.' Services are still held at the chapel, which can accommodate approximately fifty people.

ICE HOUSE AT MOFFAT
A REMINDER OF THE HYDROPATHIC HOTEL

Before the introduction of fridges and freezers and other such appliances in the 1920s, businesses and homes were forced to adopt various other means for the storing of perishable foodstuffs, or of providing ice for cooling drinks and desserts, especially during the summer. Large country houses and hotels with

The remains of the ice house in its secluded woodland setting.

The interior of the ice house.

shoals of guests to be catered for had a particularly pressing need for facilities of this kind, and often solved the problem by building an ice house.

These fascinating structures grew in popularity in Britain from about the mid-seventeenth century; designs vary from one to another, so that they come in all shapes and sizes, but the example pictured opposite is fairly typical of the usual construction: a rounded roof, not much above the surface of the land, with a brick-built chamber going deep into the earth, where the ice could be stored. For obvious reasons, ice houses were usually built near a convenient source of water.

This particular ice house, with its roof overgrown with grass and fern, is tucked away in a small wood on the edge of Moffat and would have served the vast Hydropathic Hotel. Opened in April 1878, when Moffat's reputation as a spa resort was still at its height, it was regarded as one of the largest and best-equipped hotels of its kind anywhere in Britain. The Hydro was built in a commanding position overlooking Annan Water and had 300 or so rooms. Sadly, it burned down in June 1921, but miraculously the 140 or so guests and staff who were in residence at the time escaped from the building without serious injury. These crumbling remains of the hotel's ice house are a poignant reminder of the Moffat Hydro in its heyday.

REMAINS OF MOFFAT STATION
A FRAGMENT FROM A FONDLY REMEMBERED BRANCH LINE

The branch railway line between Moffat and Beattock was opened in April 1883, and all that remains of Moffat railway station is a small building which

A remaining fragment of Moffat's former railway station.

once served as the platform toilet facilities for passengers. (A fragment of the platform itself also still survives, albeit heavily camouflaged.) Initially opened for goods traffic, it was opened to passenger trains only a month later. The journey between the two destinations, which took just six minutes, could be enjoyed for a mere 2*d*, with a return fare of only 3*d*. This compared more than favourably with the bus fare at the time, which was 6*d* for a single journey between the same two termini. The local newspaper reported that: 'By completion of the little branch line from Beattock, the fashionable watering-place of Moffat has been brought fairly into contact with the railway system, and the line cannot fail to be of great advantage to the hosts of visitors who resort to Moffat in summer.'

All of the main line trains that stopped at Beattock had connections to and from Moffat. During the late 1930s, there was even an excursion train which ran direct from Moffat to Carlisle every Saturday, leaving Moffat at 3.30 p.m. and calling at all stations en route: Wamphray, Dinwoodie, Nethercleugh, Lockerbie, Gretna, Floriston, Rockliffe and Carlisle. The train left Carlisle for the homeward journey at 10 p.m. and, with a return fare of only 1*s* 7*d*, it proved to be a very popular service.

However, the familiar shout of 'Beattock for Moffat', which guided scurrying passengers from the main line service to their branch line connection for decades, was silenced for ever in December 1954, when Moffat station and the line to Beattock were closed to passengers (although goods traffic continued on this short route until April 1964).

A WORLD RECORD HOLDER IN MOFFAT

THE WORLD'S NARROWEST DETACHED HOTEL
(AND A VERY SHORT STREET)

As befits a once-famous spa resort and a popular present-day tourist spot, Moffat is well served by hotels of differing architectural styles, including a former coaching inn and the mid-eighteenth-century building, designed by John Adam, which originally served as the Second Earl of Hopetoun's town residence. However, Moffat's most distinctive and unusual hotel must surely be the Star, if only because it has been officially recognised by the prestigious *Guinness Book of Records* as the narrowest detached hotel in the world. Designed by William Notman in 1860, the Star towers above its neighbours, and the narrow width of the red sandstone building – which measures just 20 feet from side to side – seems only to accentuate its height. The fact that the Star extends to 162 feet in length further emphasises its ultra-slim dimensions.

Chapel Street lies nearby. Connecting Star Street with Well Street, it is described locally as the shortest street in Scotland, although, where that particular record is concerned, Chapel Street would seem to have been just beaten by Ebenezer Place in Wick, which is only 6 feet 9 inches long. However, measuring a mere 18 feet 5 inches on its shorter side and being only 9 feet 11 inches wide, (not to mention comprising only one house), Chapel Street can certainly claim to be one of Scotland's shortest streets.

The Star is the narrowest detached hotel in the world.

CRUCK COTTAGE, TORTHORWALD
AN EXAMPLE OF LOCAL VERNACULAR ARCHITECTURE

During the mid-nineteenth century, records show that cruck cottages were a familiar sight in Torthorwald and represented the most common style of basic domestic dwelling and architecture in the village. There are various other forms of simple vernacular buildings to be found, such as the black house in the Highlands, for example, but the distinguishing and defining, if not unique, feature of a cruck cottage lies in its construction. The roof rests not on the walls of the building, as is usually the case, but is supported by a series of cruck frames fashioned out of sturdy oak. Although once a familiar form of basic habitation, very few examples of the cruck cottage survive intact in southern Scotland today.

A cruck cottage, Torthorwald.

The nineteenth-century missionary, John Gibson Paton, who lived with his family in a cruck cottage at Torthorwald during the 1830s, explained in his autobiography that, 'The beauty of construction was, and is, its durability, or rather the permanence of its oaken ribs! There they stand, after probably not less than four centuries, japanned with "peat reek", till they are literally shining; so hard that no ordinary nail can be driven into them.' He lamented that by the mid-1880s, 'there were only five thatched cottages in Torthorwald, where the lingering patriarchs were permitted to die slowly away.'

The interior beams of the cruck cottage.

Before the cruck cottage at Torthorwald was restored to the condition that it can be found in today, it served intermittently as an ordinary family home (after being periodically improved and refurbished), even during the later decades of the twentieth century. As so frequently happens, however, once the last occupants had departed and the cottage became empty it fell steadily into a derelict state. Work began in the early 1990s to renovate the property. The existing crucks were patched and strengthened, the walls – originally made of wattle and daub – were repaired with traditional mortar, and the roof was re-thatched with heather turf and wheat straw.

The cottage, which is currently maintained by the Cruck Cottage Heritage Association and Solway Heritage, can be viewed throughout the year. (A list of local keyholders is displayed at the cottage.)

PILLBOX AT HEATHHALL
REMAINS OF WARTIME DEFENCES

Following the spring of 1940, pillboxes appeared all around the country. They made an important contribution to the home front anti-invasion defences that were put in place at the time of what is generally regarded as Britain's 'darkest hour', when, following the evacuation of Dunkirk, the prospect of a German invasion seemed imminent.

Pillboxes were built to a variety of set designs by the War Office Directorate of Fortifications and Works, and the example pictured opposite, which is sunk into the ground and stands close to the edge of a field at Heathhall, near Dumfries, is a fairly typical one. A former wartime RAF airfield lies nearby, and so pillboxes would have been placed in this area to augment the existing defences (such as searchlight batteries etc.) that were designed to repel landings by German paratroopers.

Pillbox at Heathhall.

Just under 30,000 pillboxes were erected throughout the United Kingdom, of which it is thought that about one-fifth can still be seen today in varying states of repair. They were frequently used by members of the Home Guard (Britain's voluntary wartime defence force, memorably portrayed in the BBC television series *Dad's Army*) as training posts, but some were also employed occasionally as ammunition and weapons stores. They were often ingeniously camouflaged to blend in with their local surroundings, so that potential invaders might remain in blissful ignorance of their whereabouts. The simple intention was that, in the event of an invasion, the local Home Guard platoons would man their pillboxes and thus impede the progress of the enemy by firing from inside these makeshift strongholds.

Adrian Tierney-Jones, writing in the *Telegraph* in January 2010, to mark the seventieth anniversary of their first appearance in the British landscape, described pillboxes as the 'Norman Castles and Roman ruins of the 20th century'.

THE THEATRE ROYAL, DUMFRIES

SCOTLAND'S OLDEST WORKING THEATRE

When the Theatre Royal in Dumfries first opened in Shakespeare Street on 29 September 1792, nobody could have imagined that it would still be a flourishing enterprise over two centuries later. As such, it has achieved the enviable status of becoming Scotland's oldest working theatre (and reputedly the third oldest in Britain). It has become the home not only of the town's Guild of Players, but also accommodates the occasional touring production and hosts other theatrical and musical events.

Robert Burns was a member of the audience at the Theatre Royal in its earliest days. There was a suggestion that he might write a play to be performed there. Even though the idea did not come to fruition, he did compose several prologues that were spoken on the theatre's stage.

During the nineteenth century this 'pocket edition of a theatre', as J.M. Barrie described it, where the audience in the dress circle 'could almost shake hands with the man in the pit,' attracted some of the finest players in the land, not least Edmund Kean, who paid several visits before his untimely death in 1833. Later, his son Charles would perform on the same stage.

William Charles Macready, who became the greatest tragedian of his age, gained much vital experience at the Theatre Royal during his early days on the stage; his father leased the theatre for four years from 1813. He returned to Dumfries just before his retirement in 1845, to give performances on three successive nights as Hamlet, Shylock and Richelieu.

Barrie, who was educated in Dumfries, paid regular visits to the Theatre Royal during the 1870s. Writing many years later, he recalled the building as 'so tiny that you smile to it as a child when you go in.' He reflected on the parochial nature of a small town theatre audience. 'You find that your butcher patronizes burlesque,' he wrote, 'while your baker likes long slow deaths.' He also noted the unintentionally comic effects of under-rehearsed travelling companies, who performed four Shakespeare plays on one night with a complete change of programme the following day!

THE BURNS MAUSOLEUM, DUMFRIES
THE TALE OF A MOVING STATUE

The creamy white exterior of the Burns Mausoleum in St Michael's churchyard, in Dumfries, stands out in marked contrast to the predominantly red sandstone memorials that surround it. (In fact, the Mausoleum is also built of the local stone but overlaid with paint.) Originally, Robert Burns was buried in a simple grave nearby, but in September 1817, twenty-one years after his death, the poet's

The Burns Mausoleum in St Michael's churchyard, Dumfries.

remains were transferred to this imposing Grecian Temple-style building. Not only Burns himself, but also his widow Jean, together with several other members of their immediate family, are entombed in the Mausoleum. The foundation stone of this striking monument (designed by Thomas Hunt of London) was laid in June 1815, and the work took two years to complete. The curious feature of the Mausoleum concerns the marble figure of Burns, which originally depicted him standing behind the plough (with his muse Coila presiding over him as a backdrop). It was sculpted by Peter Turnerelli and installed at the time of the Mausoleum's completion.

Exposed as it was to the elements, the region's wet and windy climate caused the statuary to deteriorate over the years, and, in 1936 (a quarter of a century after the group had last been repaired), the figures were entirely renewed – again in marble – by Hermon Cawthra, who made a significant alteration in the process. He re-worked the piece, with Burns now shown standing in front of the plough instead of behind it. Protection from the elements is supplied by stout glass doors.

In a strange epilogue to this tale, after Turnerelli's original statue of the poet had been removed from the Mausoleum, it was displayed for a time in Burns House nearby. Later, it turned up in a local builder's yard but subsequently disappeared from view. It would no doubt be the source of much jubilation for Burnsians everywhere, were the figure ever to surface again.

The marble figures of Burns and his muse, Coila.

THE OBSERVATORY, DUMFRIES

A MUSEUM BUILDING WITH ITS OWN FASCINATING HISTORY

The Observatory, standing high above the town on Corbelly Hill, has graced the Dumfries skyline for so long that many 'Doonhamers' no longer give it a second thought. The old adage that 'familiarity breeds contempt' probably contains at least a grain of truth here, although in many cases 'contempt' may be too strong a word. However, on investigation, its history may in fact prove to be quite rewarding.

The Observatory actually started life as a windmill during the late 1700s, and it was ideally placed for the wind to drive its heavy sails. Nevertheless, the windmill's original function proved to be fairly short-lived. As the town's historian William McDowall picture-

The Observatory, Dumfries.

squely phrased it, '[The] familiar landmark, that ... like a gigantic bird flapped its wings on Corbelly Hill, seemed in 1834 about to drop away, fatally disabled by the archer Time.'

However, help and a solution were at hand. Local shipowner Robert Thomson galvanized support for the creation of what was to become the Dumfries and Maxwelltown Astronomical Society, while noted local architect Walter Newall of New Abbey was drafted in to convert the old windmill into an observatory. A telescope was duly installed, together with a camera obscura which gave – and still gives – panoramic views over the town and beyond. The Dumfries camera obscura is one of only three such instruments of its type in Scotland, and is thought to be the oldest still in operation in the world.

Nowadays, the eighteenth-century former windmill tower is part of the town's museum, which has been built around it.

LINCLUDEN ABBEY

ECCLESIASTICAL REMAINS WITH AN UNUSUAL LANDSCAPE FEATURE

The picturesque remains of Lincluden Collegiate Church – Lincluden Abbey as it is known locally – lie on the edge of a large post-war housing estate to the north of Dumfries. The tranquillity of the original setting, where Cluden Water meets the River Nith, endures to this day. The ancient abbey was a favourite haunt of Burns during his riverside rambles, and the ruins were immortalized in his song 'Minstrel at Lincluden'.

Originally established in the twelfth century as a priory for Benedictine nuns, Lincluden was extensively rebuilt and developed during the fourteenth and fifteenth centuries. A new choir was built, together with domestic quarters to accommodate a college of canons and their provost. The remains we see today date from that period, and reflect some of the finest late medieval architecture to be found among the religious houses of Scotland. The handsome choir contains the impressive tomb of Princess Margaret, who was the daughter of King Robert III of Scotland and the widow of the Fourth Earl of Douglas (who numbered among his other titles the Lordships of Annandale and Galloway). At the side of the tomb a beautifully decorated doorway leads from the choir into the sacristy.

Lincluden fared no better than other religious houses during the Reformation and, by the end of the sixteenth century, the church had fallen into disuse. The domestic quarters fell into private hands and, among other alterations and improvements made to the property and grounds, the new occupier created a knot garden, which was a landscape feature much in vogue at the time. However, within a century, Lincluden's fortunes had declined to such an extent that the crumbling buildings were being used as a quarry for stone.

The knot garden has now been restored to some extent, and provides the remains of Lincluden Abbey with one of its most unusual features.

The tomb of Princess Margaret (and the door to the Sacristy) in the Choir of Lincluden Abbey.

The partially restored knot garden at Lincluden Abbey.

THE HERMITAGE AT FRIARS CARSE
A POET'S WOODLAND RETREAT

Unobtrusively tucked away in Crow Wood, the Hermitage lies in the extensive grounds of what is nowadays the Friars Carse Country House Hotel, at Auldgirth. It is only a short step across the fields from Ellisland, where Robert Burns lived with his family from 1788 to 1791. A discreet sign, positioned beside the road leading to the hotel, points the way to this quaint and modest building which stands sheltered among trees and enclosed by railings (although there is a gate for access). With its slate tiles and crow-stepped gables, the Hermitage of the present day is actually a reincarnation of the building that Burns was in the habit of using occasionally as a peaceful retreat where he could write, at the invitation of his friend and patron Captain Robert Riddell, who owned the estate in the poet's day.

Riddell built the original Hermitage in his grounds in 1786 and, two years later, Burns immortalized it in his aptly-named poem 'Verses in Friars Carse Hermitage'. He inscribed the lines 'Thou whom chance may hither lead/Be though clad in russet weed … ' on a windowpane in the small building, but the glass was later removed to a safer place; wisely perhaps, given its obvious appeal to the less scrupulous treasure-hunter!

Burns moved away from Ellisland to Dumfries in 1791 and Riddell died in 1794. As the years passed, the Hermitage fell into decay until it eventually became derelict. The present building, which dates from 1874, stands on the same secluded site and preserves the spirit of its predecessor. In memory of Burns's standing as a staunch freemason, and in recognition of the poet's connection with the original Hermitage, Thomas Nelson, a later occupant of Friars Carse who designed the new building and arranged for it to be built, thoughtfully incorporated some Masonic symbols in the exterior stonework.

Left: *The 'Hermitage', in the grounds of Friars Carse.*

Above: *A Masonic symbol on the exterior stonework.*

THE AULDGIRTH INN

A FORMER SANCTUARY FOR CHRISTIAN PILGRIMS

Christian pilgrims and wayside inns have been linked in the public imagination since at least the fourteenth century, when Geoffrey Chaucer famously assembled his motley crew at the Tabard Inn, Southwark. It was from here that the Knight, the Pardoner, the Wife of Bath and the rest of his fictional company set off on a pilgrimage to the shrine of St Thomas Becket at Canterbury Cathedral.

A connection with this worthy tradition can be found at Auldgirth, which lies approximately eight miles north of Dumfries. Here, the village pub has served as a coaching inn and a smithy in the course of its long history. With its origins thought to stretch back to the sixteenth century, the building was conveniently placed to provide overnight accommodation for the monks of Melrose Abbey. They stayed at Auldgirth when making the long journey west from their home in the Borders to visit the shrine of St Ninian at Whithorn. Indeed, it is believed that the building we know today as the Auldgirth Inn was originally built by the monks of Melrose Abbey themselves, to serve not only as a resting place but also as a sanctuary for prayer during their long pilgrimages. The monks also appear to have established at least one other connection with the local area, because it seems they were granted the use of land at nearby Dunscore during the Middle Ages.

Visitors to the Auldgirth Inn today will find that its ancient religious connection is still recalled by the small crosses inscribed on each side of the central chimney stack, and which are a distinctive feature on the exterior of the building. The arched windows are a further reminder of the Auldgirth Inn's early connection with the monks of Melrose Abbey, and their pilgrimages into distant Galloway.

The Auldgirth Inn. The crosses on its chimney stack recall an ancient religious connection.

COURTHILL SMITHY, KEIR MILL
BIRTHPLACE OF THE PEDAL-DRIVEN BICYCLE

On the whitewashed wall of Courthill Smithy at Keir Mill, about a mile south of Penpont, there are several plaques marking the often disputed achievement of Kirkpatrick Macmillan (1812-1878), who, like his father before him, worked as a blacksmith in this quiet spot. It is widely accepted that in this small smithy, Macmillan built the world's first pedal-driven bicycle in or around 1840. He soon put his invention to the test by cycling to Glasgow and back, reputedly taking two days over the 130-mile round trip. Given the poor state of the roads in those times, and the fact that the wheels were made of wood with iron rims, this was no mean feat on Macmillan's part.

It is thought that Macmillan was inspired to build his model after seeing the early nineteenth-century hobby-horse in action – a rather basic contraption, propelled by the simple expedient of the rider's feet hitting the ground as he ran along with the 'horse' between his legs. Macmillan improved on this idea with the ingenious arrangement of a treadle on the front wheel, a crank on the rear wheel and connecting rods linking the two. It was certainly crude by modern-day standards, but the principle of pedal-driven cycling, which we now take for granted, was firmly established.

Macmillan neglected to patent his invention, and, as was inevitable, it was soon being widely produced by the hands of others; all of which led to

Above: *Courthill Smithy, Keir Mill. The home of Kirkpatrick Macmillan.*

Right: *The plaque on the wall of the smithy.*

IN THIS SMITHY
THE FIRST BICYCLE
WAS BUILT BY THE
INVENTOR

KIRKPATRICK M^CMILLAN
ABOUT THE YEAR
1840

claims and counterclaims about the true origins of the pedal-driven bicycle. Nevertheless, Macmillan is still generally given the credit as its inventor.

Commercial manufacture of the pedal-driven bicycle did not begin until after Macmillan's death in 1878. Although his original model no longer exists, a replica can be seen in the Scottish Cycle Museum at Drumlanrig. A red sandstone plaque, placed on the wall of the smithy by the National Committee on Cycling to mark the centenary of Macmillan's invention, concludes: 'He builded better than he knew.'
(Note: Courthill Smithy is not open to the public).

RETAINING WALL AT ENTERKINFOOT
AN IMPRESSIVE FEAT OF CIVIL ENGINEERING

Lying at the junction of Enterkin Burn and the River Nith, the aptly-named hamlet of Enterkinfoot is situated about six miles north of Thornhill. It is tucked into a deep gorge carved out by the Nith, at a point where the A76 trunk road from Kilmarnock to Dumfries and the Thornhill to Sanquhar stretch of the Glasgow-Kilmarnock-Gretna (Nith Valley) railway line run adjacent to each other, as they squeeze through this narrow aperture. The massive retaining wall pictured here lies only a short distance north of Enterkinfoot, and is thought to have been built by German engineers in around 1848. Even the largest of container lorries that thunder past this imposing structure are dwarfed by the wall's sheer size and presence as it uncompromisingly sweeps down to the verge of the carriageway. Not surprisingly, this impressive feat of civil engineering was considered to be the benchmark of its type when it was initially constructed.

The basic principle of a retaining wall is simple enough. In this instance its function is to guard against the effects of soil erosion and any ground movement, thereby keeping the steep-sided bank – along the top of which, on a high and narrow shelf, the railway line runs – secure and stable.

The line served by the retaining wall at Enterkinfoot is still very much in use today for passenger and goods traffic. It was opened in 1850 and originally operated by the Glasgow and South Western Railway (which eventually became a part of the London, Midland and Scottish Railway). The line provided an alternative route to Caledonian Railway's (also later absorbed into LMS) service from Carlisle to Glasgow via Beattock Summit.

The retaining wall at Enterkinfoot.

SANQUHAR POST OFFICE
THE OLDEST WORKING POST OFFICE IN THE WORLD

In 1966, a search was launched to discover Britain's oldest post office. Likely candidates appeared from far and wide. The sub-office at Shipton-under-Wychwood in Oxfordshire, for example, had occupied the same premises since 1845, making it the oldest one in England. However, it was the small Upper Nithsdale town of Sanquhar that eventually claimed the title. At first glance, the narrow-fronted post office in Sanquhar's busy high street may seem unremarkable, until you notice the date '1712' painted above the door, making it the oldest working post office not only in Britain, but throughout the world.

Of course, Sanquhar's long association with the post office predates, by many years, the introduction of uniform Penny Postage in 1840, which subsequently opened the way to a wide range of postal counter services, not least the sale of postage stamps themselves. Even so, it was not until 1897 that a postal delivery service was established to every house in Great Britain, as a gift from Queen Victoria on the occasion of her Diamond Jubilee. (Prior to that, delivery services were erratic and more or less at the discretion of the local postmaster.)

When the post office at Sanquhar was first opened, it is unlikely that it consisted of more than a small room, and its sole purpose would have been for the delivery and collection of letters by mounted 'post boys' (some of whom, in fact, were quite elderly men), who carried the mail during the years before the introduction of the mail coach service in 1784.

Even today, the post office at Sanquhar still manages to retain its old world charm, despite the fact that it is sandwiched between modern shop fronts and a busy road brushes its doorstep. Understandably, it is sought out by countless visitors from home and abroad, and by many a footsore walker on the Southern Upland Way (a long-distance footpath which passes through the town), who can't resist the opportunity of taking a look inside, or of sending a holiday postcard from the oldest working post office in the world.

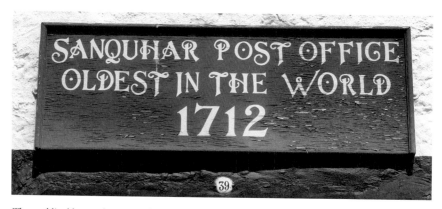

The world's oldest working post office is in Sanquhar.

SWEETHEART ABBEY

AND THREE WOMEN IN A BOAT

The considerable red sandstone
remains of Sweetheart Abbey
('supremely beautiful in decay,' as
the Dumfries historian McDowall
described them) dominate the
village of New Abbey, and loom
large above the rooftops as you
make your way through the
narrow and winding main street.
The Cistercian monastery was
founded in the second half of
the thirteenth century by Lady
Devorgilla, daughter of Alan, Lord
of Galloway, in memory of her
late husband John de Balliol who
died in 1268. The story of her love
for him is a curious and affecting
one. After her husband's death, she
carried his embalmed heart in an
ivory casket that accompanied her
everywhere.

When Lady Devorgilla herself
died in 1290, she was buried in
the abbey with her husband's
heart placed beside her, and
thus the religious house she had
founded – originally called New
Abbey to distinguish it from its
mother house, the 'old' abbey at
Dundrennan – came to be known
by the community of monks who
inhabited it as Sweetheart Abbey.

Not far from the remains of the
abbey, the eagle-eyed visitor will
notice two small stone carvings inserted into the wall of a low terraced cottage,
dating from the mid- to late eighteenth century and fronting the village's main
street. Executed in a primitive or folk art style, and painted mostly in black
against the whitewashed wall, these unusual carvings consist of a red rose motif
and three figures, with their heads covered, seated in a rowing boat. Although
difficult to understand the reason for it, given the abundance of red sandstone

The remains of Sweetheart Abbey.

Above & below: *Stone carvings on
a cottage wall, New Abbey.*

to be found locally, the carvings are said to commemorate the tireless efforts of three devoted women (their appearance in the boat is reminiscent of nuns) who reputedly worked long and hard during the construction of the abbey, transporting materials across the Solway Firth.

PRESTON CROSS & WREATHS TOWER
A 'LOST BURGH' AND A ROYAL LEGEND IN THE PARISH OF KIRKBEAN

Today, all that is left of the once-sizeable village of Preston is a weathered sandstone cross enclosed in a low circular wall at the rear of East Preston Farm. Our knowledge of Preston's history is scant, despite the village being given the rather grand title of a 'Bugh of Regality' in the 1660s. Samuel Arnott, in his *Antiquities of Kirkbean*, published in 1895 (DGNHAS Transactions), noted that, 'According to one account, it had the privilege of holding three, and according to another four fairs annually.' Preston is also believed to have had its own jail, suggesting that it was once a community of some size. Now it is often referred to as the 'Lost Burgh', the population having dwindled to only one by the early 1840s. The cross – probably once the village market cross – was unearthed and erected on its present site around 1850, having previously lain buried for some years.

To the west, about a mile across country from Preston Cross, lie the remains of Wreaths Tower, rising out of the flat surroundings like a lone jagged tooth. (It is also sometimes referred to as Wreaths Castle.) Only a fragment still exists of this probably early sixteenth-century building. It was originally quite extensive but now comprises little more than what appear to be the remains

Preston Cross.

Wreaths Tower.

of a corner stairwell rising up through several floors. Samuel Arnott wrote: 'No doubt the prevalent vandalism which deemed these old buildings the most convenient and suitable quarries for building material is responsible for much of this and, on examining the "dry dykes" which are in the vicinity, many stones, which appear to have formed part of the old castle, are to be seen.'

Arnott went on to mention the local legend that Mary, Queen of Scots rested overnight at Wreaths Tower when making her way south from Glasgow into England, following the Battle of Langside in 1568, but it is hard to establish whether this was true or not. However, as it is reported that she stayed at Terregles Castle before spending her last night in Scotland at Dundrennan Abbey (after which she crossed the Solway Firth to Workington), Wreaths would not have been immediately in her path.

ORCHARDTON TOWER
SCOTLAND'S ONLY ROUND TOWER HOUSE

Stone-built Orchardton Tower, a mile or so south of Palnackie, enjoys the unique distinction of being the only circular tower house in Scotland. Now in a ruined condition, the style of this cylindrical building should not be confused with those Iron Age structures known as brochs, which can bear a superficial resemblance at a quick glance.

Orchardton Tower was built by the Cairns family, and dates from the late 1400s. In common with countless other Scottish tower houses dating from this and later periods (and constructed in various shapes and sizes), it was intended to be not only a residence but also a fortification, so that it had a defensive purpose as well. Subsequently, Orchardton Tower passed into the hands of the Maxwell family in the early years of the seventeenth century, eventually being sold to the Douglas family in the late eighteenth century.

Orchardton Tower, near Palnackie, is Scotland's only circular tower house.

Despite the fact that it is now roofless, Orchardton Tower has a remarkably well-kept air, as do the ruined outbuildings. Originally, these would have been contained within a fortified enclosure, and would have included stables, a brew house, a bakehouse and a kitchen, together with a great hall and sundry other quarters for guests and servants. A storage cellar, the main living room (with its large fireplace and decorative piscina) on the ground floor, and the laird's bedroom above it were all contained within the tower itself. It is possible to climb to the top of the tower by means of a steep and narrow stone spiral staircase. A head for heights is essential, but the view from the top of the wall over the surrounding country makes the climb well worth the effort.

A Scheduled Monument in the care of Historic Scotland, Orchardton Tower is open to visitors throughout the year.

THE CLOSES, KIRKCUDBRIGHT

A MAGNET FOR A ONCE-THRIVING ARTISTS' COLONY

In its heyday, during the late 1890s and for much of the first half of the twentieth century, the artistic community (or 'colony') that descended on Kirkcudbright was of a varied nature, encompassing practitioners in a wide range of different mediums: watercolourists and oil-painters, potters and sculptors, illustrators and etchers etc. Some of its members undoubtedly achieved greater recognition and more enduring reputations than others, although probably the most famous and successful artist of them all was E.A.

Hornel, who lived at the elegant Broughton House in the town's High Street. However, many of the artists gravitated to and around the historic closes – such as Greengate Close – that make such an attractive feature at the heart of old Kirkcudbright.

The crime writer, Dorothy L. Sayers, was a regular visitor to the town between the two world wars and, in her novel *Five Red Herrings* (1931), she perceptively captured the flavour of life in these unusual and distinctive byways. Her aristocratic amateur sleuth, Lord Peter Wimsey, arrives in Kirkcudbright with his loyal valet Bunter in tow, where he immediately settles into the simple life:

The entrance to Greengate Close, Kirkcudbright.

> Greatly to the regret of the hotel-keepers, he had chosen to rent a small studio at the end of a narrow cobbled close, whose brilliant blue gate proclaimed it to the High Street as an abode of the artistically-minded. His explanation of this eccentric conduct was that it entertained him to watch his extremely correct personal man gutting trout and washing potatoes under an outside tap, and receiving the casual guest with West End ceremony.

There is more than a hint of Greengate Close in this description; a spot which, with the illustrator Jessie M. King and her artist husband E.A. Taylor at its helm, was a particularly bustling hive of artistic endeavour.

LOCH SKERROW HALT
ONE OF BRITAIN'S LONELIEST RAILWAY STATIONS

Arriving at what little remains of Loch Skerrow Halt after a two-hour walk along the old trackbed from Mossdale, I could quite understand why it was regarded in its day as one of the most isolated railway stations in Britain. Two lengths of abandoned, decaying platforms (eastbound and westbound) and the walls of one of the former railway buildings crumbling into the earth, are virtually all that can be seen today, where once there stood a water tower

The remains of the former platform at remote Loch Skerrow Halt.

and signal box, a siding and railways houses. The halt was on a 'passing loop' section (where the otherwise single track was double) on the old Port Road line running from Dumfries to Stranraer via Castle Douglas and Newton Stewart. The line, which closed in June 1965, is still remembered affectionately as the 'Paddy' because services from Dumfries to Stranraer met ferries to and from Ireland.

The position of derelict Loch Skerrow Halt is as remote as ever it was, lying beside the loch which gives the station its name, and surrounded by largely unpopulated rolling moorland. Passengers alighting from and boarding trains at the halt were few, except for fishermen using the adjacent loch. The hint of a literary connection is attached to Loch Skerrow Halt. Richard Hannay, the hero of John Buchan's novel *The Thirty-Nine Steps* (1915), reputedly got off a train here, having left London hurriedly, fearing that he might be the prime suspect for a couple of murders which he did not commit. He headed for Scotland and arrived 'at Dumfries, just in time to bundle out and get into the slow Galloway train … I got out … at a little place whose name I scarcely noted, set right in the heart of a bog.' However, apart from Buchan's mention of 'the single line', the station where Hannay boarded a train back to Dumfries the following day also has echoes of Loch Skerrow Halt: 'The moor surged up around it and left room only for the single line, the slender siding, a waiting room, an office, the stationmaster's cottage. There seemed no road to it from anywhere, and to increase the desolation, the waves of a tarn lapped on their grey granite beach half a mile away.'

THE TEMPLE

AN EIGHTEENTH-CENTURY FOLLY WITH A GOTHIC FLAVOUR

Follies come in many different shapes and sizes – fake towers, sham castles, mock Grecian Temples – and tend, by their very nature, to be eccentric, decorative and often ornate in appearance, although usually lacking in genuine practical purpose. In Britain, they grew in popularity from towards the end of the eighteenth century and proliferated thereafter. This was at a time when an appreciation of landscape for its own sake was increasingly being informed by, for example, William Gilpin's notions of the 'picturesque'. Follies dotted here and there often served to enliven a landscape and make it more diverting.

One of the genre's less flamboyant and more secluded examples can be found tucked away in woodland adjacent to the A75 trunk road south of Gatehouse of Fleet, and a short distance from the Cally Palace Hotel (formerly Cally House, one of Galloway's most impressive mansions). This roofless folly, with its battlements and faux windows, takes the form of a small Gothic-style temple, and was built in the grounds as a ruin in 1778 by the owner of the estate, James Murray of Broughton.

After visiting the extensive grounds of Cally House in 1792, the writer Robert Heron described it in his *Journey through the Western Parts of Scotland*, as having 'to accidental observation … all the effect that might be produced by a genuine antique.' The owners of follies often had them erected in such a position that they could be seen from home. Therefore, when it was first built, the temple could be glimpsed in the distance by the occupants of Cally House, but it has since been obscured by trees. Heron reported that, at the time of his visit, the building was actually occupied by a 'farm servant'. The man, who must have been a hardy soul indeed, apparently stayed for some years before moving to nearby Gatehouse of Fleet.

The folly built by James Murray of Broughton as a Gothic-style temple.

VIADUCTS OVER LOCH KEN
AND BIG WATER OF FLEET

FEATS OF CIVIL ENGINEERING ON THE PORT ROAD LINE

Among the many reminders scattered throughout the region relating to
Dumfries and Galloway's impressive railway heritage, these two viaducts are
particularly fine examples. They can both be found along the route of the former
Port Road line, which linked Dumfries and Stranraer. Both viaducts were in
service for just over 100 years, from the opening of the line in March 1861 until
its closure (as a part of the Beeching cuts) on 14 June 1965. The distinctive
Loch Ken Viaduct, with its soaring wrought-iron spans, carried trains over the
narrowest point of the loch on the stretch of line between the former stations of
Parton and New Galloway (the latter actually being situated at Mossdale). The
viaduct is reputed to be the oldest surviving bridge of its kind in Scotland.

Further west, the twenty-arch Big Water of Fleet Viaduct, which straddles
the river of that name, is a dominant feature in the remote country around
Dromore. There is no doubt that the overall appearance of the stone-built
viaduct – nearly 1,000 feet long and reaching to almost 100 feet at its highest
point – was somewhat marred in 1940, when every arch was strengthened with
substantial brick cladding. This was done to ensure that the structure would
bear the weight of the heavily-laden munitions trains that passed across it at
regular intervals during the Second World War. The viaduct has been used
as a film location on several occasions, including for the 1978 remake of the

Loch Ken Viaduct.

The Big Water of Fleet Viaduct.

film of John Buchan's novel *The Thirty-Nine Steps*. It could also be seen in the 1975 television adaptation of Dorothy L. Sayers' Lord Peter Wimsey tale, *Five Red Herrings*, whose convoluted plot unfolds in the surrounding Galloway landscape. A nearby nine-arch viaduct that crossed the Little Water of Fleet on the Port Road line was blown up by the army after the route had been closed, but – like the Loch Ken Viaduct – the Big Water of Fleet Viaduct has been spared so far.

MULBERRY HARBOURS
THE LINK BETWEEN GARLIESTON AND THE D-DAY LANDINGS

Walking south from Garlieston, along the coastal footpath that winds its way down to the village of Isle of Whithorn, it is hard to imagine that Rigg or Cruggleton Bay – a haven of tranquillity for those in search of peace and quiet – once played an important role in helping to shape the course of events during a critical stage in the Second World War.

There are several reminders from that time dotted along this stretch of the coastline. Look out into the bay, and you will see what, at first glance, appears to be an indistinct wreck, besieged by cormorants and other sea birds making it their playground and nesting place. In fact, these remains (which comprise part of a pontoon or supporting structure) date from a year or two before the Normandy D-Day landings of 6 June 1944, when the prototypes of three different designs of floating harbour – 'Mulberry Harbours' as they came to be known – were tested in the waters around Garlieston. The area had been

The remains of a half-submerged Mulberry Harbour at Rigg or Cruggleton Bay.

chosen as a suitable testing site due to the similarities that existed between the coastline here and that part of Normandy where the floating harbours were eventually to be deployed.

In due course, two completed artificial, mobile harbours, whose numerous sections had been manufactured at various points around the British Isles and assembled near Lee-on-Solent in Hampshire, were towed across the English Channel by an army of tugs. Once they arrived at the Normandy coastline, the Mulberry Harbours were destined to effect the swift unloading of allied troops, supplies and munitions just prior to D-Day itself. It is difficult to visualise the enormity of these floating structures; each one of the pair that made its way to the French coast was said to be almost the size of Dover Harbour, once it had been assembled.

CHAPEL FINIAN

A REMOTE SHELTER FOR WEARY PILGRIMS

Travelling north-west along the coastal road from the fishing village of Port William towards Glenluce, the remains of Chapel Finian can be found near Corwall Port on the edge of Luce Bay. It is an exposed and windswept spot, which is thought to have once served as a landing place for pilgrims arriving by boat from Ireland, on their way to visit the shrine of St Ninian at Whithorn. If that were indeed the case, it would explain the existence of the small and simple chapel, constructed in a style often to be found in Ireland, set in this sparsely populated and remote area of Galloway. On the other hand, however, it fails to explain why such pilgrims did not choose to sail only a short distance further east along the coast and disembark closer to their intended destination.

Chapel Finian was probably named after a sixth-century Irish saint, who became a noted Christian missionary and spent some time studying at Candida Casa, the church established by St Ninian at Whithorn. As a teacher, he numbered the future St Columba among his pupils. The neat ruins that can be seen today, which clearly show the outline of the small rectangular chapel itself, together with a wall around the perimeter, are thought to date from the tenth or eleventh century, and may be the successor of an even earlier building constructed at this isolated place.

The remains of Chapel Finian, on the edge of Luce Bay.

In 1684, the Revd Andrew Symson, Minister of Kirkinner, referred to it as 'a little ruinous chapel, called by the countery [*sic*] people Chapel Finzian' in his book, *Large Description of Galloway*. Although little of the original building now remains, Chapel Finian does retain a particularly interesting feature from its ancient past: the stone-lined well that, in all probability, supplied water for the priest's domestic quarters. The well can be clearly seen lying close to the roadside drystone wall that encloses the remains of Chapel Finian.

CABLE HOUSE NEAR PORTPATRICK
EARLY UNDERWATER COMMUNICATIONS
BETWEEN SCOTLAND AND IRELAND

Tucked away at the foot of Dunskey Glen, a mile or so north of Portpatrick, the Laird's Bay (or Port Kale) Cable House is an evocative reminder of a bygone age. In fact, the building is made up of two separate huts joined together, which were constructed at different times. In more recent years, this rundown property was used as a Coastal Interpretation Centre, but when it was originally built, a single hut accommodated one end of the telegraph cable that was laid under the sea between the mainland of Scotland and Ireland during the 1850s. 'It would be difficult to find a more picturesque situation for a cable hut than Port Kail Bay [*sic*] … on the Wigtownshire coast of the Irish Channel' wrote John G. Bell in the magazine, *St Martin's-le-Grand*, in 1899.

The Laird's Bay (or Port Kale) Cable House at the foot of Dunskey Glen, near Portpatrick.

Remnants of old cable can still be found lying on the beach nearby.

There had been earlier attempts to establish communication by telegraph between Scotland and Ireland but, as Bell explains, 'it was not until 1854 that the first cable was successfully laid from Black Head, at the entrance to Belfast Lough, to Sandeel Bay (or Port Mora), about one-and-a-quarter miles north of Portpatrick Harbour, and some 200 yards from the present site of Port Kail [*sic*] cable station.' Bell went on to explain that, prior to 1870, one hut had been sufficient 'for the accommodation of the [subsequent] four-wire telegraph cables stretching from Donaghadee, and Whitehead in Belfast Lough, to Port Kail [*sic*]'. However, in 1893, a telephone cable was also laid, and a second hut was added to the original building to accommodate it. Another cable house was built a couple of miles further north along the coast at Knock, but it has long since disintegrated, and there is little to show that it ever existed.

Meanwhile, at Laird's Bay the disused cable house still bravely rides out the brutal south-westerly gales, and provides a useful excuse for weary walkers to pause a moment on their trek along the 212 miles of the Southern Upland Way footpath, which meanders past these quaint twin buildings.

4

Objects and Artefacts

THE TELFORD ARCH

AN APPRENTICE PIECE BY A FAMOUS CIVIL ENGINEER

Thomas Telford was born the son of a shepherd in very poor circumstances at Westerkirk, near Langholm, in 1757. By the time of his death in 1834, he had achieved enormous success and international fame, not only as a civil engineer and architect, but as a prolific builder of canals, bridges and roads. (His friend, the poet Robert Southey, amusingly dubbed him the 'Colossus of Roads'.)

Evidence of Telford's numerous and varied works can be found far and wide. For example, by the age of thirty, he had been appointed Surveyor of Public Works in Shropshire where, during the course of his tenure, he constructed more than forty bridges. Later, after assisting with the rebuilding of London Bridge, he became the engineer responsible for the building of the Caledonian Canal, which links the east and west coast of Scotland, and also for the Menai Suspension Bridge, between Anglesey and the mainland of Wales.

Above & below: The Telford Arch, Langholm, with its inscribed plaque.

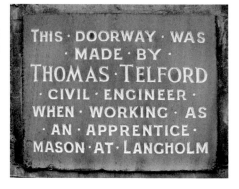

Telford's career began humbly enough. After being unsuccessfully apprenticed to a stonemason at Lochmaben, he was taken on by a new master at Langholm, where he finally completed his apprenticeship. In those days, according to one of Telford's biographers, 'Langholm was then a very poor place, being no better in that respect than the district that surrounded it. It consisted chiefly of mud hovels covered with thatch.'

However, from the late 1760s, the principal local landowner, the Duke of Buccleuch, began to implement systematic improvements to local houses, roads and bridges, resulting in Telford finding himself fully employed once his apprenticeship had been completed. The Telford Arch, comprising two pillars with an arched top and crowned by a stone ball, is a relic from his days as an apprentice, and originally served as a doorway at Langholm's old King's Arms Hotel. Now it stands, somewhat incongruously perhaps, against a wall on a small patch of green beside the High Street.

THE RUTHWELL CROSS
A RELIC OF THE DARK AGES

For more than 125 years, the Ruthwell Cross has held centre stage in the parish church at Ruthwell, where the 18-feet high column dominates its purpose-built apse. Dating from the seventh or eighth century, the cross, whose panels are decorated and carved with scenes from the life of Christ, and with lines from the Old English poem, 'The Dream of the Rood', is regarded as probably Scotland's finest Dark Age runic monument.

Its origins are unclear. It is not known who made it or precisely when it was executed, but it was certainly hewn from local stone. It was probably used at first as a preaching cross, placed out of doors at a spot where people would assemble to worship in the days before a church was built on the site. When a stone-walled church was eventually built at Ruthwell, it was constructed around the cross and left partly unroofed to accommodate its height. In this way, the monument remained intact for centuries.

The Ruthwell Cross, standing in its purpose-built apse.

However, during the religious upheaval of Charles I's reign, the General Assembly of the Church of Scotland ordered that the cross should be destroyed as it was deemed an 'idolatrous object'. It was broken up into sections and buried in the earthen floor of the church, and there the pieces stayed, until they were dug up during excavation work in the 1780s. Fortunately, the Revd Henry Duncan, Ruthwell's minister from 1799, recognised the historical and religious significance of the remains and, with the help of skilled craftsmen, was eventually able to reassemble the cross (although it became necessary to add a new crossbeam as the original was never found). After restoration work was completed in 1823, the Ruthwell Cross was erected in the garden of the manse where, for over sixty years, it stood exposed to the full force of the elements in that unsheltered coastal landscape. In 1887, the cross was moved back inside the church, where it has remained ever since.

DUNCAN'S CHAIR

THE BIRTH OF THE SAVINGS BANKS MOVEMENT AT RUTHWELL

The Revd Henry Duncan, minister of Ruthwell from 1799, is generally credited as the founding father of the savings banks movement which began, to all intents and purposes, when Duncan opened his first ledger on 10 May 1810, in the whitewashed cottage that stands at one end of Ruthwell's main street, and which is now the Savings Banks Museum. It is here that the heavy wooden chair in which Duncan sat when receiving his parishioners' savings can now be seen. It was specially made for him by local estate workers in 1815 at a cost of 18s 6d.

Duncan's scheme was a simple one. In his struggling agricultural parish, where a farm labourer's daily wage was barely a shilling, he collected from the villagers those tiny amounts of money they could just afford to part with once their basic needs had been met. Later, he deposited the cash with the Linen Bank in Dumfries. At a time when the minimum deposit required by most, if not all, banks was £10, making it impossible for ordinary working people such as the agricultural labourers of Ruthwell to ever open an account of their own, the advantages of Duncan's simple plan were obvious. At the end of each financial year, he redistributed the amounts saved, together with the interest earned over the previous twelve months. It was on the commercial principal of the Ruthwell scheme that the savings banks movement flourished, and grew into the force that it subsequently became.

By 1818, more than 130 similar small savings banks, each of them operating along the lines of Duncan's Ruthwell model, had grown up in Scotland alone, with many more having opened in England and Wales. The first American bank to emulate Duncan's scheme opened in Philadelphia in 1916 and for many years

The chair that was specially made for the Revd Duncan by local estate workers in 1815.

bore the Duncan tartan on its passbook. Ruthwell's savings bank closed in 1876, and all the accounts were subsequently transferred to nearby Annan.

THE LINCLUDEN RHINOCEROS
UNUSUAL ROADSIDE ANIMAL SCULPTURE

Readers of a certain age may recall a memorable scene in the once highly popular BBC TV sitcom *Hi-De-Hi*, set in a 1950s holiday camp, in which, while enjoying some liquid refreshment on the beach, the irascible and alcoholic Punch and Judy man, Mr Partridge, watches a horse being given a piggyback ride across the sands by another horse. Fearing that he might be hallucinating, Partridge seeks further solace in the bottle. (In fact, it is a pair of pantomime horses whose occupants are indulging in some innocent horseplay!)

That scene often comes to mind when I drive through Lincluden to the north of Dumfries, where, close beside the A76 trunk road, you will find a mock bus shelter surmounted by the figures of a fibreglass adult rhinoceros and its calf. The origins of this startling spectacle lie back in the 1980s, when suggestions were invited from the local community for ways in which to enliven the appearance of the area. With the child's natural gift for imaginative thinking, pupils from local schools were drawn to the novel idea of placing a rhinoceros on top of a much-used bus shelter. Their dreams were made real, courtesy of a generous arts grant and the expertise of artist Robbie Coleman.

Subsequently, the rhino on the Glasgow Road garnered a great deal of interest, not least from those passengers who used the bus stop in question. However, with the advent of the Dumfries bypass, the bus shelter and its attendant rhino were removed to make way for a roundabout. The rhino

The Lincluden Rhinoceros.

was safely put into storage, but a clamour by local townspeople for it to be reinstated resulted in the construction of the mock bus shelter that we can see today. It was at this stage that the calf was added to the sculpture. Returning home through Lincluden after a late night out in town, you could easily be forgiven for thinking – like poor old Mr Partridge – that you are hallucinating.

A PRISON ARCH & UNUSUAL ORDNANCE
INTRIGUING DISCOVERIES IN THE GROUNDS OF DUMFRIES MUSEUM

The grounds of Dumfries Museum harbour several items of particular interest. On entering from Primrose Street and climbing the steps, the visitor will pass through a low stone arch that once served as an entrance to one of the town's former jails, which stood close by the Tolbooth on the east side of the High Street. It was built in 1583; only a decade or so before Parliament made it compulsory for every burgh to have its own prison sufficiently secure enough to 'detain all persons who break His Majesty's laws'. Prior to that date, the detention and punishment of miscreants had been haphazard in the extreme and varied enormously from one place to another.

The building remained in use for a surprisingly lengthy period of time, serving as a place of incarceration throughout the seventeenth and eighteenth centuries. When a large part of the jail was damaged by fire in 1742 it was

rebuilt. However, as McDowall explains in his *History of Dumfries*, 'So increasingly insecure had the prison become with the lapse of years, and so defective was it in other respects, that the county and burgh authorities resolved in 1801 to erect a new one.' The jail was demolished in 1808 but, fortunately, the historic arch has been preserved.

Elsewhere in the museum grounds, a cannon stands unobtrusively beside a hedge. Referred to as the Russian Gun, it is reputedly a relic of the Crimean War, captured and brought home as a souvenir, probably by men of the local King's Own Scottish Borderers. It was installed in the museum grounds around 1880, some time after the present Greyfriars Church was built; prior to which the cannon had stood approximately in the position that Burns's statue now occupies.

Above & below: *Stone arch and the Russian Gun in the grounds of Dumfries Museum.*

At one time, the Russian Gun was attended by two Carronades, thought to be made by the Carron Iron Company of Falkirk in the 1770s. Alfred Truckell, a former Curator of Dumfries Museum, wrote that they were the prototypes of Patrick Miller of Dalswinton. 'It was his idea to arm naval vessels with many small guns and to this end he commissioned the Carronade … As such, they are unique as their dimensions were not eventually adopted.' These two unusual pieces of ordnance can now be found in Dock Park.

THE 7STANES
UNUSUAL SCULPTURES IN FOREST SETTINGS

There is little doubt that, over the past twenty-five years or so, mountain biking has become one of this country's most popular forms of physical recreation, enjoyed by people of all ages. The forest paths and tracks of Dumfries and Galloway provide an ideal environment in which to pursue this pastime and, to that end the 7Stanes mountain biking centres have been established in the region at Glentrool, Kirroughtree, Dalbeattie, Mabie and Ae. Here, riders can test their skills on trails that cater for all levels of ability and experience; from the most gentle to suit the beginner, to the more extreme routes for the most hardened and expert of riders.

Visitors out cycling, walking or horse riding along or close to these trails, cannot fail to be intrigued by the highly individual sculptures – there is one located at each of the 7Stanes centres – that they may encounter along the way, including the 'Ghost Stane' in Mabie Forest and the 'Talking Head Stane' in Ae Forest. Three further sculptures can be found at 7Stanes centres in the region: the 'Giant Axe Head' at Glentrool, the 'Gem Stane' at Kirroughtree and the 'Heart Cleft Stane' at Dalbeattie. (Beyond Dumfries and Galloway, in Borders Region, the 'Meteorite' can be seen at Glentress and the 'Border Stane' at Newcastleton).

The seven large sculptures were created and executed by a team led by Carlisle-born artist Gordon Young. The enigmatic 'Ghost Stane', which weighs over two tons and stands in a sheltered spot by a stream in Mabie, is made from white marble.

The 'Ghost Stane' in Mabie Forest.

The 'Talking Head Stane' in Ae Forest.

Close inspection reveals that it is engraved with a lace pattern. At Ae, the rather more striking 'Talking Head Stane' (weighing over one-and-a-half tons) rests beside a track in an exposed position high above the forest. In addition to the usual, if somewhat exaggerated, facial characteristics, the head, carved from a granite boulder, is inscribed with lines translated from a Scandinavian poem: 'But still it satisfies my/Soul to hear the spruce and the wind/They speak together like sister and brother/And use such beautiful wild wind words/Deep in the forest, deep in the forest.'

IRON YETTS AT BARJARG TOWER
PRISON GATES IN AN UNUSUAL SETTING

It is difficult to imagine what could possibly link 'Annie Laurie', one of the world's greatest and most famous love songs, with a set of gates – or more properly in this instance, yetts – that are said to have once been in service at the old nineteenth-century prison in Buccleuch Street, Dumfries. The unlikely connection between the two is the seventeenth-century Barjarg Tower, situated south-east of Keir Mill, where Anna Laurie was born in 1682. She became known as Annie Laurie to the world at large after being immortalized in a song that is thought to have been largely based on a poem written by her erstwhile

Iron yetts at the south-eastern entrance to the grounds of Barjarg Tower.

suitor, William Douglas. (Nowadays, Annie Laurie herself is perhaps more closely associated with Craigdarroch House, near Moniaive, where she lived after her marriage to Alexander Fergusson, Laird of Craigdarroch, in 1709.)

Frequently found in Scotland, yetts were typically openwork or lattice-style iron gates that were used in buildings such as castles, royal palaces and prisons; anywhere, in fact, where high security was of the essence. The plain iron yetts at Barjarg now form a part of the nineteenth-century gatehouse, situated at the south-eastern entrance to the grounds of the tower house. Accepting, as local legend suggests, that the yetts did come from the old Dumfries Prison built in 1802, they must have been installed at their new – and present – site some time after the Buccleuch Street jail was demolished in 1883.

GLENCAPLE AND CARSETHORN
SEAFARING REMINDERS OF TWO COASTAL VILLAGES

Situated on either side of the River Nith, a few miles apart, the coastal villages of Carsethorn and Glencaple were once thriving outports of Dumfries. Glencaple formerly boasted a considerable shipbuilding trade, in addition to being an important port of call, where vessels sailing as far afield as America and the West Indies could take on and discharge their cargoes. One ship, the

Duchess of Buccleuch, built at Glencaple in 1835, was wrecked off the coast of Cuba during a voyage from Bristol to Havana in 1842. All the crew survived, but most of them subsequently died of fever.

James King Hewison writes in his book *Dumfriesshire* (1912) that, 'Glencaple in 1840 boasted of a shipbuilding yard where two vessels of over sixty tons burden were built annually. But the advent of the railroad destroyed

The boat-shaped bench in the garden of the Steamboat Inn, Carsethorn, bears the names of emigrants bound for Prince Edward Island in 1774-5.

The remains of the pier at Carsethorn.

all this local business; timber, goods and cattle being transferred to the railway.' By the 1880s, Groome's *Ordnance Gazetteer of Scotland* was declaring that Glencaple's 'shipbuilding is all but extinct; and ranking as a sub-port of Dumfries, it has scarcely any trade of its own, but serves for such vessels to discharge their cargoes as are unable to sail up to [Dumfries].'

An inscription carved into one of the wooden boat-shaped benches, which are placed at intervals along the roadside at Glencaple, records that in the village's heyday, 'Enough tea leaves were landed here to make fourteen million cups of tea,' and that, 'Enough tobacco leaves were landed here to fill seven hundred and fifty million pipes.' An inscription carved into another bench lists the names of all the ships that were built at Glencaple between 1806 and 1858, while the inscription on a third bench commemorates the final voyage of the *Duchess of Buccleuch*.

This boat-shaped bench at Glencaple is carved with the names of the vessels built in the village between 1806 and 1858.

At Carsethorn, another boat-shaped oak bench can be found placed in the garden of the Steamboat Inn. During the eighteenth and nineteenth centuries, thousands of emigrants left from Carsethorn in search of more prosperous lives in North America, Australia and New Zealand. (Convicts from Dumfries Prison who were sentenced to transportation also left from here.) The bench at Carsethorn is inscribed with the names of passengers who boarded the *Lovely Nelly* in 1774 and 1775, bound for what is now called Prince Edward Island. Joiners, weavers, blacksmiths and farriers were just some of the trades of those men hoping to find employment in Canada.

A pier was built at Carsethorn in 1840 by the Nith Navigation Commission, to accommodate incoming and outgoing vessels. It was on this structure that the emigrants took their last few steps on their native soil. The decaying wooden posts of the old pier can still be seen today.

THE GALLOWS KNOB

A GRIM RELIC AT THREAVE CASTLE

Simply paying a visit to Threave Castle is something of a curiosity in itself. A ten-minute walk through farmland from the car park at Kelton Mains brings you to a jetty. Here, you must ring a bell to summon the custodian, who will then ferry you across to the castle which stands on an island in the middle of the River Dee. Apparently, the level of the river was higher in former times than it is today, thus making the island smaller than it is now. Nevertheless, the castle still retains its air of splendid isolation.

Built in the late 1300s by Archibald 'the Grim', the Lord of Galloway, who became the Third Earl of Douglas, the remains of Threave Castle are of intrinsic merit in their own right. However, for devotees of the macabre, the ruined fourteenth-century keep possesses a feature of particularly chilling fascination. Look up, high above the main front door of the building and you will see, perched at the top of the wall, a small piece of protruding stone known as the 'Gallows Knob', or the 'Hanging Stone', which once formed part of an ancient gallows. It was from this spot, exposed to the full public gaze, that the Douglases despatched their enemies and miscreants in general. As Malcolm Harper explained in his *Rambles in Galloway* (1876):

> The Douglases were a haughty, powerful race; and [Threave Castle] was the seat and centre of a grinding despotism that stretched over the whole district of Galloway. William, Eighth Earl of Douglas, asserting his superiority over all the other nobles in the south of Scotland, haughtily boasted to Lord Herries at the commencement of their well-known feud in 1452, that the 'Gallows Knob' of Threave had not been without a

The jetty on the approach to Threave Castle.

The 'Gallows Knob' at Threave Castle.

tassel [a body hanging from it] for the last fifty years. It is said that, lest this barbarous emblem of feudal power should at any time want its usual decoration, some unoffending vassal was tucked up when no malefactor was in readiness.

FONT AT THE SELKIRK ARMS, KIRKCUDBRIGHT
ECCLESIASTICAL FURNITURE IN A HOTEL GARDEN

As Gloucestershire poet Ivor Gurney declared in his poem *Cotswold Ways*, 'One comes across the strangest things in walks'. It was a line that occurred to me when I first discovered an octagonal stone font resting on a large circular stone in the unlikely setting of the garden at the Selkirk Arms in Kirkcudbright. Nowadays, it makes for a rather impressive flowerpot, its presence lending a certain charm to the already attractive surroundings, and providing a guaranteed talking point for the hotel's guests.

Dating from the fifteenth century (around 1481), the font is thought to have come originally from Dundrennan Abbey, situated about five miles east of Kirkcudbright, although it is not possible to be certain about its

The font in the garden of the Selkirk Arms, Kirkcudbright.

provenance. There are various carvings on the side of the font that are somewhat difficult to interpret, largely owing to the fact that the bowl has obviously been left outside and at the mercy of the elements for much of the past few centuries. However, the images that can still be deciphered include one of a bird holding on to a fox by a tether, and the MacLellan family's coat-of-arms inscribed on a shield.

Should the font, as suspected, have once formed a part of the ecclesiastical furnishings at Dundrennan Abbey (whose buildings fell into decline from the sixteenth century), then it certainly endured a chequered history during the years that followed. It eventually arrived in the garden of the Selkirk Arms by way of St Mary's Isle, and it is reported to have served at various points along the way as a water trough and even a stepping stone.

BRUCE'S STONE

A ROYAL RESTING PLACE AT CLATTERINGSHAWS

The rather nondescript granite boulder standing on Moss Raploch, near the edge of Clatteringshaws Loch, is in the care of the National Trust for Scotland, to whom it was presented by the Earl of Mar in 1932. Known as Bruce's Stone, it has acquired great significance locally over the centuries as the rock against which the early-fourteenth century Scottish king, Robert the Bruce, is supposed to have rested, following his exertions in a victory against the English in the spring of 1307. Unfortunately, the actual spot where the skirmish took place is no longer to be seen, having been submerged when the dam was built to create the reservoir at Clatteringshaws during the early 1930s.

Robert the Bruce had already been crowned King of Scotland in 1306 at Scone, but he and his followers were swiftly defeated in a succession of battles with the army of the English king, Edward I (the so-called 'Hammer of the Scots'), rendering Bruce little more than a fugitive for a while, in this febrile period of the Scottish Wars of Independence.

Bruce's Stone on Moss Raploch, by Clatteringshaws Loch.

After lying low and marshalling his resources, Bruce turned up in the south-west of Scotland in March 1307. Following his modest victory at Clatteringshaws against a small contingent of the English army, he went on to achieve another success the next month at nearby Glen Trool.

Robert the Bruce was destined to experience many changes of fortune in the years that followed, before achieving his great victory at the Battle of Bannockburn in 1314. This paved the way to his eventual recognition in 1328, by the reigning English monarch Edward III, as king of an independent Scotland.

A formal monument commemorates the Battle of Glen Trool, in the shadow of Merrick, some miles to the west. However, the more homely Bruce's Stone has something of the human touch; literally so, if the local legend is to be believed.

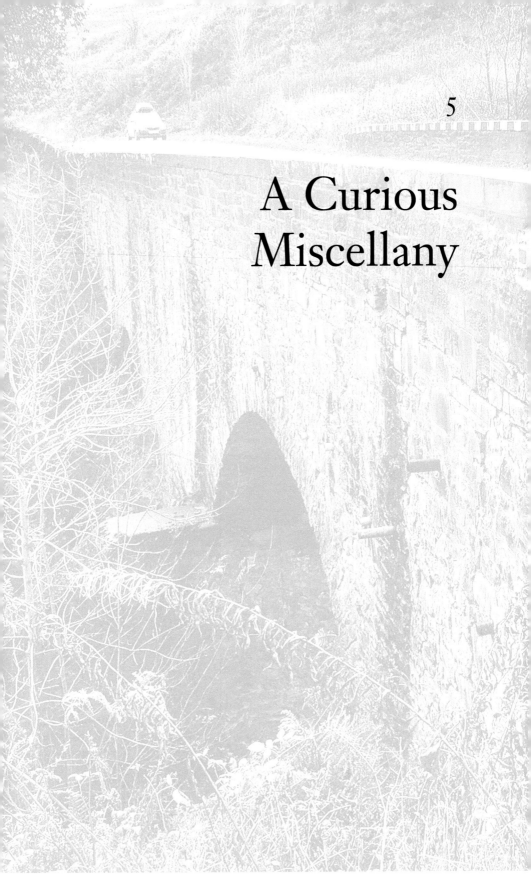

5

A Curious Miscellany

THE VENDACE

BRITAIN'S RAREST FRESHWATER FISH AT LOCHMABEN

The vendace, often described as small and herring-like in appearance, is a fish of some antiquity, dating back to the last Ice Age of about 13,000 years ago. Samuel Lewis, writing in the *Topographical Dictionary of Scotland* in 1846, described it as being 'Remarkable for a thin membrane on the top of the head, in the form of a heart, of a brownish hue and perfectly transparent, under which the brain is distinctly visible.' Regarded as something of a delicacy, the vendace is officially recognised as Britain's rarest freshwater fish, having been found at only four known sites, two of those being at Lochmaben: Mill Loch and Castle Loch, thus making the vendace in Scotland unique to Dumfries and Galloway. (The other two sites are Bassenthwaite Lake and Derwent Water in the Lake District.)

The vendace had become extinct at Mill Loch by 1970, and it seems likely that the population at Castle Loch died out well before that time. However, it was a different matter in the nineteenth century. 'A vendace club meets annually at Lochmaben in July or August,' Lewis recorded, 'and is supported by the chief gentlemen of the district.'

The vendace has not been found at Bassenthwaite Lake since the beginning of this century although, during the 1990s, vendace fry from that site were introduced with some success to Loch Skeen above the Grey Mare's Tail, north-east of Moffat and just within the boundary of Dumfries and Galloway.

Castle Loch, Lochmaben, was once home to the vendace.

This carving of a vendace can be found on a bench beside Castle Loch.

Local historian, William McDowall, reported that, during a dinner given for King James VI when he visited Dumfries in 1617,

> The harmony of the party was sadly broken in upon by James himself. Some strange little fishes – vendaces from Lochmaben – were set before him, with the intention that they were a delicacy peculiar to the neighbourhood. The King, thinking they emitted a peculiar smell, and that they had a suspicious appearance, viewed them with as much horror almost as was felt by his ancestor Macbeth when the ghost of Banquo glided in to disturb the feast at Glamis.

RUXTON'S DUMP

GRISLY REMAINS DEPOSITED NEAR MOFFAT

On 2 October 1935, the *Dumfries and Galloway Standard* reported that the local police were attempting to solve one of the most gruesome and terrible murders ever committed in the country. A few days earlier, a woman staying on holiday at Moffat was walking a couple of miles north of the town when she noticed some 'scattered articles' in the shallow bed of a stream. On later examination, the police found them to be the severed arms and legs and mutilated heads of two human bodies.

During the next few days, more than thirty packages containing human flesh and bones wrapped in newspaper were discovered in the area, leading police to believe that the murderer was someone with a working knowledge of human anatomy. The unusual nature of what came to be known in some

The bridge and ravine, north of Moffat, where Buck Ruxton disposed of his victims' remains.

quarters of the press as the 'jigsaw murders', gripped the public's imagination throughout the country as the grisly details unfolded.

Dr Buktyar Rustomji Ratanji Hakim was a Bombay-born General Practitioner who moved to the United Kingdom and, in 1930, started work in Lancaster under his adopted name of Buck Ruxton. On 15 September 1935, at No. 2 Dalton Square, he strangled his wife on suspicion that she was conducting a secret love affair. He also murdered their young housemaid, who had heard the violent exchange between the two. Ruxton then drove to a bridge about two miles north of Moffat, on the road to Edinburgh, where he disposed of his victims' dismembered remains in the ravine below; a spot which is still known locally today as 'Ruxton's Dump'. He would have become familiar with this lonely place when travelling to and from Edinburgh, where he had studied on a postgraduate course at the University.

Despite taking great pains to destroy the bodies of his wife and housemaid, Ruxton was charged and convicted of murder, largely as a result of the forensic evidence that the police were able to gather, and which enabled them to identify the victims. As such, it was one of the earliest cases of its kind. Ruxton also made the simple error of wrapping some of the body parts in a local Lancaster newspaper, thus helping to lead the police to him. He was hanged in May 1936.

WILLIAM HARE IN DUMFRIES

A NOTORIOUS MURDERER COMES TO TOWN

The story of the nineteenth-century Edinburgh serial killers, William Burke and William Hare, who sold the bodies of their victims to a doctor for dissection by his anatomy students, has become the stuff of legend. They murdered seventeen people before being apprehended by the police. However, owing to a lack of sufficient evidence to convict the pair, Hare was given the opportunity of testifying against Burke in return for his own immunity from prosecution. Burke was duly hanged in January 1829, and Hare was set free by the authorities, who proposed to send him back to his native Ireland.

Hare stayed in Dumfries on 6 February 1829, en route from Edinburgh to Portpatrick, sparking one of the largest disturbances in the town's history. McDowall, the Dumfries historian, takes up the story: 'A vast crowd, estimated at 8,000 people, collected on the streets – the greatest concourse being in the vicinity of the King's Arms Hotel, where Hare was located, awaiting the departure of the Galloway Mail, which was due to leave at eleven o'clock in the morning.' Not surprisingly, Hare stayed put in his top-floor room. McDowall concluded that had he ventured out into the street, 'All the nameless rabble of the town, from the Moat-brae to the Cat's Strand, would have torn him to pieces without mercy.'

Plaque marking William Hare's connection with Dumfries.

After several false starts and the use of decoys, Hare was smuggled out of his quarters at the King's Arms during the afternoon and, with the noise of the mob baying for his blood ringing in his ears, he was placed in the relative security of the town jail in Buccleuch Street. In the early hours of the morning of the 7th, when the crowd had dispersed, instead of travelling on to Portpatrick as originally planned, Hare was sent down through Annan into England. Little is known of his fate thereafter, although one account claims that he died in the 1860s as a blind beggar on the streets of London.

THE EXECUTION OF ROBERT SMITH
THE LAST MAN TO BE PUBLICLY HANGED IN SCOTLAND

The last public execution to be carried out in Scotland took place in Dumfries on 12 May 1868, when nineteen-year-old Robert Smith from Eaglesfield was hanged for the crimes of murder, rape, robbery and attempted murder committed near Cummertrees and Annan. A few weeks later, the Capital Punishment Amendment Act received the Royal Assent, thus bringing this grotesque spectacle to an end throughout the United Kingdom.

The day of Smith's execution dawned dull, overcast and wet, but even so, a crowd estimated at roughly 600 people gathered outside the prison in Buccleuch Street in time to witness the terrible event due to take place at eight o'clock in the morning. 'It was mostly composed of young people of the working classes,' reported the local newspaper, 'and contained more females than was at all creditable to the sex; few persons were present from the country.' The report in the *Dumfries and Galloway Standard* spared its readers no detail of the grisly occasion:

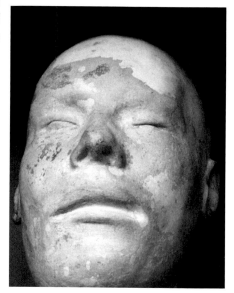

> The culprit's face was turned towards the crowd. Askern [the executioner] approached him and hurriedly drew the white cap over the head of the condemned man. Then a fearful cry issued from the crowd, many of whom turned their backs on the terrible spectacle and literally ran from the revolting scene. As motionless as a statue the unhappy youth stood upon the fatal drop, while the executioner placed the rope round his neck.

The death mask of Robert Smith.

At this point it was discovered that the noose had not been properly adjusted, so there was a slight delay while it was removed and replaced. 'What an agony of mind the poor wretch must have suffered in that brief period of suspense,' the newspaper report continued. 'The executioner then shook hands with Smith and, stepping back, drew the bolt.'

Later in the day, just before the convict was buried in the prison precincts, Mr Rushfirth, a plasterer from Carlisle, made a cast of Smith's head. This somewhat macabre death mask can still be seen in Dumfries Museum.

CLOG-MAKING
A ONCE-FLOURISHING TRADE IN DUMFRIES

This easily overlooked sign, painted on an old sandstone doorpost in Queensberry Street, Dumfries, provides an unobtrusive reminder of the town's thriving clog-making trade from bygone times. Traditional clogs – their leather uppers and wooden soles held together with nails – were a widely used form of footwear in Britain from about the late eighteenth century until just after the Second World War. Their popularity stemmed from the fact that they were considerably more durable and cost less than half the price of conventional boots and shoes. With occasional upkeep, a well-made pair of clogs could last for more than twenty years. This cheap and sturdy form of footwear was universally adopted by workers in the mines and mills of nineteenth-century industrial Britain. Within living memory, there were still clog makers in every town and almost every village throughout Dumfries and Galloway, and, together with tanning, shoemaking, basket making and fleshing, clogging added to the distinctive list of trades once practised in Dumfries.

In 1869, David Bremner, writing in his book *The Industries of Scotland*, recorded that the number of people employed in the tweed mills of Dumfries and the neighbouring area around that time was 'upwards of 1,000', and so – as with the workers in the Lancashire and Yorkshire cotton mills – the local demand for clogs was considerable.

In 1875, the town's suspension footbridge across the River Nith was completed, and it is reported that when the mill workers swarmed across it in the dusk of frosty early mornings and evenings at the beginning and end of their day's work, bright sparks from the nails in the soles of their clogs could be seen piercing the darkness.

An old shop sign in Queensberry Street, Dumfries.

CATTLE DROVING IN DUMFRIES AND GALLOWAY
A HELPFUL GUIDE AT THE MIDSTEEPLE, DUMFRIES

Many people – townsfolk and visitors alike – will pass the Midsteeple in Dumfries without giving a second glance to the interesting table of distances fixed to a wall of the building. The destinations shown on the cast-iron plate include Portpatrick, Castle Douglas, Annan and Carlisle, but Huntingdon seems rather a random choice. In fact, its inclusion was invaluable to the eighteenth- and nineteenth-century cattle drovers who gathered at the Midsteeple on their way through the town, and for whose benefit the plate was originally erected.

The naturalist and antiquary Thomas Pennant, who visited Dumfries in 1772, noted that, 'Vast droves from Galloway pass through [Dumfries] on their way to the fairs of Norfolk and Suffolk.' Stranraer, New Galloway, Kirkcudbright and Castle Douglas were among the important collection points along the route to the town. In fact, the annual total of cattle being driven south from Galloway through Dumfries numbered up to 40,000, and Huntingdon was reckoned to be one of the most important of the English markets.

However, as William McDowall recorded in his *History of the Burgh of Dumfries* (1867), such a large trade could bring its own problems. 'Droves of cattle are apt to be troublesome to the owners or tenants of the grounds near which they pass and such was the case here ... the country people endeavouring by violence to stop the droves, and impose illegal exactions of money upon the cattle.'

By the middle of the nineteenth century droving had begun to decline, as cattle were increasingly being shipped instead from various ports along the Solway Coast. 'No quarter of the kingdom has benefited so largely by steam navigation

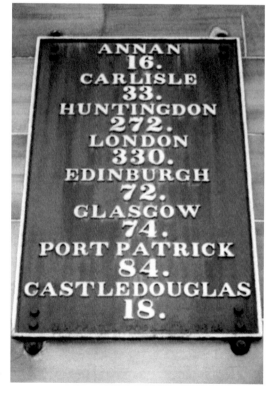

Table of distances on the wall of the Midsteeple, Dumfries.

as Dumfriesshire and Galloway,' declared *The Farmer's Magazine* in 1837, 'which, no doubt, may quietly be attributed to the moderate freights exacted in that quarter . . . which charges are not more than the expense of droving . . . ' After steam navigation there followed the development of the railways, and cattle were taken down into England by truck rather than being herded through Dumfries.

A PAIR OF FAMOUS NAVAL SONS FROM KIRKBEAN
ADMIRAL JOHN CAMPBELL AND JOHN PAUL JONES

Appropriately, perhaps, given its proximity to the coast, the tiny village of Kirkbean, lying just beneath Criffel, has nurtured two famous seafaring men. The slightly earlier – and now less famous – of the pair was Admiral John Campbell. He was born the son of the local minister around 1720 and, in the early days of his career, between 1740 and 1744, he circumnavigated the globe under the supervision of the famous English naval commander, George Anson. Campbell subsequently became a noted pioneer in the field of naval navigation, and, in 1782, towards the end of his life, he was made Commander in Chief and Governor of Newfoundland.

Meanwhile, three years after Campbell had completed his voyage round the world, the head gardener's wife on Kirkbean's Arbigland Estate gave birth to a son, in the small stone cottage that was the family's home. The boy was called John Paul. He added 'Jones' to his name during the 1770s, supposedly in an attempt to conceal his identity after killing another sailor in self-defence.

In 1761, at the age of thirteen, Jones left school and signed on for a seven-year seaman's apprenticeship. Fortune smiled on him, and he rose speedily through the ranks. After eventually leading voyages of his own to the Indies and elsewhere, he gravitated to America in the early 1770s, where he began his association with the US navy, which was then in its infancy. His subsequent naval career involved daring exploits in both the American and Russian fleets. However, his firing of the harbour at Whitehaven in 1778 during the American War of Independence (when Jones's sympathies lay with the colonists, thus bringing him into direct conflict with the British naval fleet), caused him to be regarded at home as something of a pirate. Benjamin Disraeli wrote that, 'The nurses of Scotland hushed their crying charges by the whisper of his name.'

Meanwhile, Jones worked tirelessly in the US, encouraging the authorities to raise their standards of naval training and efficiency; a crusade that was eventually to bear fruit with the founding of the Annapolis Naval College, and with Jones earning for himself the unlikely sobriquet 'Father of the American Navy'. Jones's cottage birthplace at Kirkbean is now a museum.

John Paul Jones's birthplace at Kirkbean.

John Paul Jones, by Kirkcudbright artist Tim Jeffs. This plaque hangs in the Selkirk Arms, Kirkcudbright.

THE LEADHILLS AND WANLOCKHEAD RAILWAY
BRITAIN'S HIGHEST ADHESION RAILWAY

The reconstructed section of track that forms the Leadhills and Wanlockhead Railway lies in South Lanarkshire and is, therefore, geographically beyond the scope of this volume. However, the fact that the line terminates abruptly at the small wooden platform of Glengonnar Halt, set in a deep cutting about half a mile north-east of Wanlockhead and on the border with Dumfries and Galloway, qualifies it for inclusion in these pages. (At the time of writing, it has still not proved possible to extend the line to Wanlockhead itself.)

The narrow gauge tourist railway of today follows the course of the original standard gauge trackbed, which was laid by Caledonian Railways at the beginning of the twentieth century. This carried lead from the mines at Wanlockhead and Leadhills into various other parts of the country, via its connection at Elvanfoot with the main Carlisle to Glasgow line. (This branch line was closed in the late 1930s, following the closure of the local mines.)

The section of narrow gauge track that runs from the small station at Leadhills to lonely Glengonnar Halt is distinguished by the fact that, at almost 1,500 feet above sea level, it is the highest adhesion railway in Britain. The construction of this line was begun in the 1980s by a team of enthusiastic volunteers. Today, the small brightly-painted carriages, pulled or pushed

Sign at Glengonnar Halt.

The train leaves Glengonnar Halt, bound for Leadhills.

(depending on which direction the train is travelling) by an equally small and resplendent engine, carry passengers on a short and slow journey of just over half a mile each way, through a rugged landscape of disued mine-workings in the heart of the Lowther Hills.

(Note: The Leadhills and Wanlockhead Railway operates at weekends from Easter until the end of September, but check the timetable beforehand.)

WIGTOWN

SCOTLAND'S 'NATIONAL BOOK TOWN'

Designated as Scotland's first and only 'National Book Town' in 1998, it must seem to the outside observer that, on geographical grounds alone, Wigtown is an unexpected choice of location. When the idea of Scotland's own Hay-on-Wye (Wales's 'town of books') was first proposed, and hopeful contenders from around the country invited to apply, Perth, Dunblane and Strathaven, together with Gatehouse of Fleet and Moffat (the last two situated in Dumfries and Galloway), were among those who threw their hats into the ring. When the final decision was eventually made in favour of Wigtown,

This shop in Wigtown lays claim to being Scotland's largest second-hand bookshop.

which lies in the Machars of Galloway south of Newton Stewart, it must – as the Whithorn-born poet and scholar Alastair Reid observed – have set even some Scots puzzling over their maps to find out where the place was.

In the years prior to becoming a 'Book Town', Wigtown, with its resident population of approximately 1,000, had endured a depressing period of sustained economic decline. This followed the axing of the town's railway station in 1950, and the later closure of the local Bladnoch Distillery. The whisky distillery, which is the most southerly in Scotland, has subsequently re-opened.

It was Wigtown's pressing need to reinvent itself that was instrumental in helping to secure its 'Book Town' status. Formerly, the town had been scarred with decaying and empty properties, whereas it now boasts over a dozen bookshops (one of which lays claim to being Scotland's largest second-hand bookshop), together with other thriving book-related enterprises scattered around the town and its immediate surroundings. The Wigtown Book Festival has also become an important fixture on the literary map. The former BBC reporter and Member of Parliament, Martin Bell, the actress Celia Imrie and the novelist Allan Massie have all appeared at this event in the past.

BELTED GALLOWAY CATTLE
A DISTINCTIVE NATIVE BREED

While the Lakeland fells have their flocks of native Herdwick sheep, and Exmoor and Dartmoor are known for their ponies, so Dumfries and Galloway can boast of its eponymous Belted Galloway cattle. It is a breed with such distinctive markings that, no matter where in the world it may be encountered, it could not be mistaken for any other variety.

In fact, there are three types of Galloway cattle: Galloways, White Galloways and Belted Galloways. Usually black (although they can also be of a red or dun colour), Belted Galloways are instantly recognisable by their eye-catching pure white middle. Their precise origins are shrouded in a degree of mystery, although it is most widely held that they stem from a crossing of the Dutch Belted Cow (or Lakenvelder) with the traditional Galloway, possibly about three centuries ago.

Always without horns (or 'polled', as it is known), 'Belties', as they are more affectionately called, are a familiar sight throughout their native region but they are, of course, by no means confined to this part of south-west Scotland.

A 'Beltie'.

They are a genuinely hardy breed, capable of thriving in a harsh climate and on rough ground (thus ideally suited to Dumfries and Galloway). During the winter months, 'Belties' are able to maintain their inner warmth by means of a double hair coat, which also has the immeasurable advantage of helping them to keep dry by not allowing snow or rain to penetrate. Add to this their characteristically benign nature, their reputation for producing sturdy calves, and the high quality of their lean and flavourful meat, it is not surprising that 'Belties' have attracted enthusiasts throughout the United Kingdom and around the world. The first herds to be established in the USA, for example, arrived just before the Second World War. Nowadays, herds of Belted Galloways can also be found in Europe and Canada, as well as Australia and New Zealand.

BIBLIOGRAPHY

Armstrong, Lyn, *Woodcolliers and Charcoal-Burning*, Singleton, West Sussex, Weald and Downland Open Air Museum, 1978

Gifford, John, *The Buildings of Scotland: Dumfries and Galloway*, London, Yale University Press, 2002

Harper, Malcolm M. *Rambles in Galloway*, 1876

Heron, Robert, *Journey Through the Western Parts of Scotland*, 1793

Maxwell, Sir Herbert, *The Place-Names of Galloway*, Glasgow, Jackson, Wylie & Co., 1930

MacKenzie, William, *The History of Galloway*, 1841

McDowall, William, *History of the Burgh of Dumfries*, 1867

M'Kerlie, P.H., *History of the Lands and their Owners in Galloway*, 1870

Sayers, Dorothy L., *Five Red Herrings*, London, Hodder & Stoughton, 2003

Stitt, Lisa, *Ae Village: Celebrating 50 Years*, 1997

Transactions and Proceedings of the Dumfriesshire and Galloway Natural History and Antiquarian Society (various dates)